To Be
Reformed

To Be
Reformed

Living the Tradition

Joseph D. Small

Publisher
Joseph D. Small
Editor
Mark D. Hinds

Published by Witherspoon Press, a ministry of the General Assembly Mission Council, Presbyterian Church (U.S.A.), 100 Witherspoon St., Louisville, Kentucky.

Unless otherwise indicated, Scripture quotations in this publication are from the New Revised Standard Version (NRSV) of the Bible, copyright © 1989 by the Division of Christian Education of the National Council of the Churches of Christ in the U.S.A. Used by permission. Every effort has been made to trace copyrights on the materials included in this book. If any copyrighted material has nevertheless been included without permission and due acknowledgment, proper credit will be inserted in future printings after notice has been received.

Library of Congress Control Number: 2010927777

Contents

For past and present colleagues in the Office of Theology and Worship

Chip Andrus
John Burgess
Harold Daniels
Paul Detterman
Barry Ensign-George
Quinn Fox
Aurelia Fule
Paul Galbreath
David Gambrell
Theo Gill
Kris Haig
Dennis Hughes
Stephany Jackson
Nalini Jayasuriya
Robert Johnson

Dick Junkin
Brad Kent
Kim Long
Debbie McKinley
Martha Moore-Keish
Kevin Park
Jack Rogers
Steve Shussett
Valerie Kiriishi Small
Sheldon Sorge
Teresa Stricklen
George Telford
Tammy Wiens
Charles Wiley
Gláucia Vasconcelos Wilkey

I thank my God in all my remembrance of you . . . because of your partnership in the gospel from the first day until now.
Philippians 1:3, 5

Preface

A book is a mysterious object, I said, and once it floats out into the world, anything can happen. All kinds of mischief can be caused, and there's not a damned thing you can do about it. For better or worse, it's completely out of your control.

Paul Auster, *Leviathan*[1]

Every organization needs a measure of clarity about what it is and what it intends to do. Ford Motor Company, the American Red Cross, Metro-Goldwyn-Mayer, and the Pittsburgh Pirates all need to be clear about their core mission, about goals that move them toward fulfillment of their mission, and about objectives that provide markers on the way to meeting those goals. Churches are no different. If they are to avoid purposeless drift or passive reaction to forces around them, congregations and denominations alike must articulate a vision of who they are, what they are to do, and how they are to do it.

Why, then, are organizational "vision statements" so banal, and goals and objectives so tedious? Perhaps more important, why do they so seldom make a real and enduring difference in the identity and activity of organizations? Sometimes mission statements, goals, and objectives simply state what an organization is already doing (or imagines it is doing), in which case there is no need to pay attention to them. Sometimes they are worded at such a high level of generality and abstraction that they cannot function as guides to changed thought and action. Sometimes they simply express a sense of what the organization lacks, voicing a longing for something that cannot quite be identified.

Several years ago, the Presbyterian Church (U.S.A.) adopted a "Mission Work Plan" of goals and objectives. The four goals—evangelism, justice, vocation, and discipleship—were so broad that they could mean almost anything to anyone. The Church also approved a brief list of objectives that was intended to provide some measure of specificity. One of these was "Reformed identity." The objective had a wistful air about it, for it did not aim to strengthen an already robust Reformed identity among members. Instead, the objective recognized the widespread lack of a cohesive sense of what it means to be *Reformed* Christians within the multitude of Christian traditions and churches in North America. The objective identified a problem.

American Presbyterians are not alone in their limited grasp of the Reformed tradition. The World Alliance of Reformed Churches (WARC), representing nearly three hundred Reformed churches worldwide, has recognized the same problem. A major theme of a recent WARC General Council was "Reformed Self-Understanding: Who Are We Called to Be?" The General Council's primary recommendation was to "encourage member churches to study what it means to be Reformed in their own contexts," and to "prepare study texts to be used at the congregational level regarding the basic elements of Reformed thought and life."[2] Would member churches have to be encouraged to study what it means to be Reformed if they already understood and approved the basic elements of Reformed thought and life?

Over a decade ago, I wrote a book that was intended to introduce the Reformed tradition's perspective on Christian faith and life. *God and Ourselves: A Brief Exercise in Reformed Theology* proved useful enough to ministers and study groups that the publisher asked if I would rework the book, providing a revised edition for publication. I agreed, thinking that the task could be accomplished quickly. However, when I dusted off the manuscript and began to identify needed alterations, it soon became apparent that more than revision was needed. In the years since the publication of *God and Ourselves*, my understanding of the Reformed tradition and its relevance to contemporary life has been considerably broadened and deepened. Rather than a revised edition, I needed to write a new book.

Since *God and Ourselves*, my understanding of Reformed faith and life has been broadened by greater acquaintance with the Dutch Reformed tradition, lived out in our culture by the Christian Reformed Church (CRC) in North America and the Reformed Church in America (RCA). This theological and ethical stream has enriched my thinking, and I hope not only that this book reflects my appreciation, but that it will be useful in CRC and RCA contexts.

My understanding has also been broadened by sustained exposure to the increasing body of work by women theologians within the Reformed tradition, exemplified by a remarkable collection of essays in *Feminist and Womanist Essays in Reformed Dogmatics*.[3] Wide reading and conversations with Reformed theologians Leanne Van Dyk, Cynthia Rigby, and Laura Smit have been particularly important to me. I have also been enriched by significant works from Reformed racial and ethnic perspectives, including writings such as Gayraud Wilmore's *Black and Presbyterian*,[4] Allan Boesak's *Black and Reformed*,[5] Justo and Ordina González's *Christianity in Latin America*,[6] and Choan-Seng Song's *Jesus, the Crucified People*.[7] Works such as these broaden the tradition beyond its European male origins.

Deepened understanding has come from continued reading and conversations with a wide range of Reformed thinkers. Important writers and colleagues are too numerous to name, but I want to recognize two persons whose too-early deaths I continue to grieve. Colin Gunton of Great Britain and Lukas Vischer of Switzerland blessed me with incisive writing, illuminating conversations, and enduring friendships that I miss greatly. The theological and liturgical work of my colleagues in the Presbyterian Church (U.S.A.) Office of Theology and Worship, past and present, has always enriched my own work, challenging me with new questions and strengthening me with new insights. I am particularly indebted to my wife, Valerie. A Presbyterian elder, she is a keen interpreter of Scripture and an insightful theologian who always inspires me to think beneath the surface, and who usually understands when I disappear into my study.

I quote extensively from Reformed theologians throughout this book. I do this, in part, to exemplify the *tradition*. John Calvin receives considerable attention, not because he is a privileged authority, but because his life and work have been a formative influence with continuing relevance for Reformed churches. Karl Barth is quoted frequently, not because he is always right, but because his thinking is so often squarely within the ongoing Reformed tradition. Other theologians are also cited, of course, and the influence of still others who are never quoted is present throughout.

Contemporary novelists have also contributed to my thinking about Christian faith and life. Writers of deep religious conviction, of ambiguous conviction, and of no religious conviction offer perspectives that go beyond the conventional. The brief fictional excerpts that introduce each chapter are not mere ornamentation; they frame what follows in creative, suggestive ways.

So, *To Be Reformed* is not just *God and Ourselves 2*. Its structure owes much to *God and Ourselves*, and portions of some chapters are revisions of the earlier book, but I trust that the substance of *To Be Reformed* is broader and deeper, and I hope that it will be more useful to the church's ministers, elders, deacons, and members.

A Note on Theology and Language
A few comments about language may be helpful to readers. The English language has developed in ways that sometimes express gender exclusivity, employing masculine nouns and pronouns to refer to all people. The Presbyterian Church (U.S.A.) recognizes this problem and acknowledges that the diversity present in both church and world is not always reflected in the language of the church. "Definitions and Guidelines on Inclusive Language," adopted by the 197th General Assembly (1984) and reaffirmed by the 212th General Assembly (2000), provides guidance that helps the church overcome the linguistic limitations embedded in English-language expressions of the Christian tradition.

The church's policy is clear that every effort should be made to use inclusive language with respect to the people of God. In reality, inclusive language for the people of God is no longer controvertible in most parts of the church. The church's clear commitment has even helped us to understand that the original inclusivity of some biblical, creedal, and liturgical texts has been masked by gender-exclusive English translations! As with everything that I write, this book is fully gender inclusive in every reference to God's people.

Language for God presents a more difficult problem. "Definitions and Guidelines" is clear that our language for God should be as intentionally diverse and varied as that of Scripture and tradition. "Definitions and Guidelines" is also clear that the Trinitarian designation "Father-Son-Spirit" is not to be altered, although it may be supplemented. (I say more about Trinitarian language in Chapter 4.) Among other things, this means that the prominent biblical and creedal terms "Father" and "Son" are to be used, not avoided, although they should not be employed exclusively or excessively.

The problem of language for God becomes particularly difficult with pronouns. The English options are *he, she,* and *it.* Use of *it* and *itself* would be inappropriately impersonal, thus leaving us with a choice between masculine and feminine pronouns. "Definitions and Guidelines" recognizes the problem, suggesting the use of nouns rather than pronouns—for example, "God shows God's love" rather than "God shows his love." Some writers substitute passive for active voice, as in "God's love is shown." Others eliminate the pronoun: "God shows love."

The English language does not lend itself to natural solutions. The church's legitimate concern for inclusive language sometimes has the unintended consequence of depersonalizing our talk about God and each other. Use of the passive voice removes God as an active, personal presence in the world. God's love is shown . . . by whom? Eliminating the pronoun lacks specificity. God shows love . . . a generic quality? The mechanical substitution of "God" for "he," and "God's" for "his," leads to abstract, impersonal, tedious language that renders God abstract, impersonal, and tedious.

The weakness of the pronoun-to-noun strategy would be obvious if non-theological writing employed it. As I write this, I am reading Michael Ondaatje's novel, *In the Skin of a Lion.* At the beginning of the narrative, Ondaatje describes the thoughts of a young boy, Nicholas, as he wakes up on a cold winter morning—"He longs for the summer nights, for the moment when he turns out the lights, turns out even the small cream funnel in the hall near the room where his father sleeps." Imagine instead, "Nicholas longs for the summer nights, for the moment when Nicholas turns out the lights, turns out even the small cream funnel in the hall near the room where Nicholas's father sleeps." Alternatively, consider what would happen to a passage from Anne Tyler's novel, *The Accidental Tourist,* if Macon's name were substituted for every use of the third-person masculine pronoun: "Still, Macon noticed Macon had a tendency to hold Macon's arms close to Macon's body, to walk past furniture sideways, as if Macon imagined the house could barely accommodate Macon. Macon felt too tall. Macon's long, clumsy feet seemed unusually distant. Macon ducked Macon's head in doorways." The depersonalizing drumbeat repetition of "God" and "God's" is especially problematic in worship, where impersonal abstraction suggests a merely generic deity.

I confess that I do not have a good solution, particularly in the case of pronouns. I try to work around the limitations of English grammar and syntax, but there are times, especially when indicating God's active engagement in the world, when the use of masculine pronouns seems unavoidable. At those points, I can only trust that we all know God is beyond gender. God is neither male nor female, but rather the One who declares, "I am God, and not a human being—the Holy One among you" (Hosea 11:9, TNIV).

Appreciation

Finally, a word of appreciation for Witherspoon Press editor Mark Hinds, whose perceptive critique and wise suggestions have made this book better than it would have been without him.

---

1. Paul Auster, *Leviathan* (New York: Penguin Books, 1992), p. 5.
2. Milan Opocenský, ed., *Debrecen 1997: Proceedings of the 23rd General Council of the World Alliance of Reformed Churches* (Geneva: World Alliance of Reformed Churches, 1997), p. 184.
3. Amy Plantinga Pauw and Serene Jones, eds., *Feminist and Womanist Essays in Reformed Dogmatics* (Louisville: Westminster John Knox Press, 2006).
4. Gayraud S. Wilmore, *Black and Presbyterian: The Heritage and the Hope* (Philadelphia: Geneva, 1983).
5. Allan Boesak, *Black and Reformed* (Maryknoll, NY: Orbis Books, 1984).
6. Justo and Ordina González, *Christianity in Latin America* (Cambridge: Cambridge University Press, 2008).
7. Choan-Seng Song, *Jesus, the Crucified People* (Minneapolis: Fortress Press, 2001).

Why Reformed?

The history of the church is very complex, very mingled. I want you to know how aware I am of that fact. These days there are so many people who think loyalty to religion is benighted, if not worse than benighted. I am aware of that, and I know the charges that can be brought against the churches are powerful.

Marilynne Robinson, Gilead[1]

Some denominations in North America regularly encounter a puzzling phrase to characterize their churches—"the Reformed tradition." It may seem odd, in a time when many church members move easily from one denomination to another, to stress the particularity of a specific ecclesial tradition. Is the emphasis on the Reformed tradition an anxious response to widespread confusion about denominational identity and purpose? Are churches grasping at the Reformed tradition in an attempt to establish a niche boutique in the Protestant shopping mall? Whatever the reason for the renewed emphasis, the strategy may not be sound. We live in a time and place that is not receptive to tradition of any sort, especially a tradition that places a claim on our personally shaped faith and life. Even if we are open to the possibility of tradition, why should "Reformed" be reserved for Presbyterian churches and denominations such as the Reformed Church in America and the Christian Reformed Church, whose very names claim identity with the tradition? Are not all Protestants heirs of the sixteenth-century Reformation?

Mixed motives may lie behind the current use of "Reformed tradition," but the expression is not new. *Reformed* has been used for centuries to designate one of the four major streams of the Protestant Reformation: Lutheran, Anabaptist, Anglican, and Reformed. In this narrower sense, Reformed churches are those bodies that grew out of the Reformation in Switzerland, following the spiritual and intellectual lead of Ulrich Zwingli in Zurich and John Calvin in Geneva. The Reformed family of churches and their shared tradition are not named after their founder (as in Lutheran), or a distinguishing practice (as in Anabaptist), or the location of their establishment (as in Anglican). Perhaps this lack of specificity indicates vagueness, for the Reformed tradition is the most diffuse of the ecclesial movements emerging from the sixteenth-century Reformation in Europe. A certain lack of precision has characterized Reformed churches from the outset: Zurich and Zwingli on the one hand and Geneva and Calvin on the other are related yet distinct origins of the Reformed stream. Before "Reformed" could even be called a tradition, Calvin and Heinrich Bullinger, Zwingli's successor in Zurich, had to negotiate a fragile agreement concerning their differing views on the Lord's Supper. Since then, the Reformed tradition has been characterized by diversity, finding expression in presbyterian and congregational forms of governance, liturgical and free church worship, a high view of the Sacrament of Baptism and Eucharist and sacramental minimalism, doctrinal precision and individualistic convictions.

In North America, churches with Reformed ancestry cover a broad range of convictions and practices, and most embody some form of the tensions that have been present from the outset. Tendencies are detectable. Churches with Dutch and Scottish roots, such as the Christian Reformed Church, the Reformed Church in America, and the Presbyterian Church (U.S.A.), find Calvin congenial. Churches with English roots, such as the United Church of Christ, are likely to be more Zwinglian. Other churches with Reformed roots are no longer self-consciously or identifiably Reformed, including many Baptist denominations and the Christian Churches of the Stone-Campbell movement.

Confessing the Faith, Reforming the Church

Why are these churches and the tradition they embody called "Reformed"? The name derives from a distinctive appreciation of what it means to confess the faith, and a characteristic understanding of the role of confessions in reforming the church. From the beginning, churches that followed the lead of Zwingli and Calvin were characterized by the conviction that each church is called to confess the faith *in tempore* and *in loco*—in its particular *time* and *place*. Early expressions of the Reformation throughout Switzerland were marked by citywide disputations between advocates of reform and Catholic representatives, resulting in formal civic decisions to adopt church reform. The Ten Theses of Berne (1528) is an early instance of Reformed confession. The first two theses declare,

I. The holy Christian Church, whose only Head is Christ, is born of the Word of God, abides in the same, and does not listen to the voice of a stranger.
II. The Church of Christ makes no laws or commandments apart from the Word of God. Hence all human traditions, which are called ecclesiastical commandments, are binding upon us only in so far as they are based on and commanded by God's Word.[2]

Berne's strong affirmation of Christ's sole lordship over the church, and of the sole authority of Scripture in the church, set the tone for Reformed confessions throughout the churches in the Swiss cantons.

As the influence of the Swiss reformation spread, churches were established in France, Germany, the Netherlands, Hungary, Scotland, England, Poland, Italy, and beyond. These new churches generated confessions of faith as expressions of both the freedom and the obligation to proclaim the gospel in their own contexts. In the sixteenth century alone, Reformed churches produced more than sixty confessions of faith.[3] In the twentieth century, more than twenty-five churches adopted new confessions.[4] Because of the profusion of personal, local, and national confessions in the sixteenth century, the early Reformed Christians were dismissively called "the confessionalists."

The number and variety of Reformed confessions is not simply an accident of history and geography. Multiple confessions grow from a firm conviction about declaring the faith, coupled with alertness to the danger of reliance on a particular declaration. In addition to the Reformed obligation to confess the faith in each time and place, Reformed churches have been acutely aware of the dangers of idolatry, including the idolatry of exalting creeds and confessions above their status as secondary authorities, subordinate to Scripture. Thus, the tradition has understood that every particular confession is open to discussion, and that discussion may lead to theological enrichment or even to confessional modification. In this way, time- and place-specific confessions can be clarified or supplemented by subsequent statements, made in other times and places. Commitment to a living confessional tradition is the reason that sixteenth-century attempts to join all Reformed churches in one common confession, or to produce a "harmony" of all Reformed confessions, were unsuccessful, and why an early twentieth-century discussion of the desirability and possibility of a universal Reformed confession found few supporters. Reformed churches have almost never identified a single historic confession as *the* authoritative expression of Christian faith for *all* times and places.

The Reformed stance toward confessing the faith is evident in the statement of Heinrich Bullinger at the signing of the First Helvetic [Swiss] Confession in 1536:

> We wish in no way to prescribe for all churches through these articles a single rule of faith. For we acknowledge no other rule of faith than Holy Scripture. . . . We grant to everyone the freedom to use his own expressions which are suitable for his church and will make use of this freedom ourselves, at the same time defending the true sense of this Confession against distortions.[5]

There have been times when particular Reformed churches have embraced a single historic confession to express their faith and guide their action—often the Westminster Confession of Faith; even then it was understood that confessional practice entails the recognition of confessional mutability. Westminster itself attests that "all synods or councils since the apostles' times . . . may err, and many have erred; therefore they are not to be made the rule of faith and practice, but to be used as a help in both."[6] The insight of the second thesis of Berne—"all human traditions . . . are binding upon us only in so far as they are based on and commanded by God's Word"—continues to mitigate confessional authority. Nevertheless, confessions remain essential components of the church's faith and life, for it is through confession of core beliefs, as an aid to faith and practice, that a Reformed church defines for itself and declares to the world "who and what it is, what it believes, [and] what it resolves to do."[7]

These characteristics—distrust of a single confession; freedom to express the one gospel in diverse ways; focus on the particular needs of churches in different contexts—lead to the continuing Reformed practice of confession making. Churches belonging to the Reformed family have been disposed to state their deepest convictions in every generation, often, but not always, in formally adopted confessional statements. This Reformed distinctive is stated succinctly in the Presbyterian Church (U.S.A.)'s Confession of 1967. The preface begins with the conviction that "the church confesses its faith when it bears a present witness to God's grace in Jesus Christ." This need for *present* witness is a necessary feature of the church's life, and so, "in every age, the church has expressed its witness in words and deeds as the need of the time required. . . . No one type of confession is exclusively valid, no one statement is irreformable."[8]

Within the Reformed tradition, the confessional witness of each church in its own time and place is understood to be a vital aspect of the continuing reform of the church. Before a church can confess faith, the church must first listen, for it is in hearing the Word of God that the church's faith and life are questioned and renewed. Faithful listening to God's Word is essential to ensuring that a church's confession is shaped by the gospel rather than by its own interests. Because self-absorption is a corporate as well as a personal possibility, churches must measure their faith and life by the norm of God's Word: Does the church speak and act in obedience to Jesus Christ, under the authority of Scripture?

Even as a particular church listens expectantly and then speaks faithfully, it should not imagine that its confession of faith belongs to itself alone, or that its contextual witness takes place in isolation from other churches. The church in each place is bound to churches in other places by deep patterns of mutual responsibility, and thus no one church should act unilaterally. At its best, the Reformed tradition's deep commitment to the catholicity of the church encourages shared witness, not solitary declaration. A striking instance of the Reformed sense of mutual responsibility and accountability can be seen in the preface to the Scots Confession of 1560. The church in Scotland was pleased "to have made known to the world the doctrine which we profess and for which we have suffered abuse and danger," but it was not content simply to announce its confession. Thus, the preface goes on to request that

> . . . if any man will note in our Confession any chapter or sentence contrary to God's Holy Word, that it would please him of his gentleness and for Christian charity's sake to inform us of it in writing; and we, upon our honor, do promise him that by God's grace we shall give him satisfaction from the mouth of God, that is, from Holy Scripture, or else we shall alter whatever he can prove to be wrong.[9]

This "testing" of confessional witness within a wider community of churches is a guard against the parochialism that imagines one church's time and place to be the only time and place that matter.

North American churches are privileged to hear contemporary Reformed confessions of Christian faith that are voiced in contexts that differ from our own. Their very difference informs and challenges our confession in our own context. A dramatic case in point is the Confession of Belhar from South Africa. During the depths of the racial apartheid system, the Dutch Reformed Mission Church—a small, predominantly "coloured" church—declared its theological opposition to the division of Christians along racial lines. Its vision of Christian unity bears dramatic witness to the gospel's call for racial unity, but it extends to the overcoming of all divisions within the body of Christ:

> We believe . . . that unity is, therefore, both a gift and an obligation for the church of Jesus Christ; that through the working of God's Spirit it is a binding force, yet simultaneously a reality which must be earnestly pursued and sought: one which the people of God must continually be built up to attain.[10]

American Christians may not live in officially segregated churches, but racial separation remains a reality in too many congregations and denominations. Other forms of ecclesial separation are also painfully obvious. Few Christians deny that Christ's people should be one, and many even pay lip service to the search for the visible unity of Christ's church. Yet ecumenical understanding is too often restricted to a "spiritual unity" that is content to live comfortably with enduring ecclesial division and subdivision. Can our easy acquiescence to church division—racial, economic, theological, moral, and more—be challenged by Belhar's proclamation of the gospel imperative to unity?

A different and perhaps less comfortable confession comes from the Presbyterian-Reformed Church in Cuba. Its 1977 Confession of Faith acknowledges that the church's life is challenged by Cuba's communist context, but that (perhaps ironically) Marxists inspire Christians to fresh readings of Scripture:

> The Scriptures teach us that the human being is characterized by being an "econome" of all things, God's "steward." All goods, material and spiritual, that we obtain as persons or as nations, cannot be considered in the final analysis as "individual" or "national" property in an exclusive way, be it individualistic, classist, elitist, or nationalistic.[11]

The language may sound alien to American ears, and some may even suspect that the Cuban church's witness has been distorted by its context. Nevertheless, we may be challenged to think through the tension between our conventional testimony that "all that we have is Thine alone, a gift, O Lord, from Thee" and our easy assumption that what we have is ours to do with as we please. In turn, we may wish to challenge the Cuban confession's reading of Scripture, but we do not have to agree with it in all respects in order to be confronted by the fact that *our* cultural context is centered on buying and selling rather than distributing and sharing, on individual gain rather than communal well-being. Does *our* context also influence our reading of Scripture? Can our reading of Scripture be deepened by receiving insights that come from the readings of others?

The church's contemporary context is a necessary element in the authentic articulation of its faith and life. Receiving present witness does not mean discarding previous witness, as if we, in our time and place, have reached the pinnacle of Christian knowledge and church life. Those who have lived and died the faith before us have Christian wisdom to share with us, insights that can expand our horizon and deepen our comprehension of God's Way in the world.

The value of voices from the past may be appreciated in a sixteenth-century French confession from "the churches dispersed in France." These Reformed churches were not powerful or secure; they were a small minority living under the shadow of threatened or actual persecution. Perhaps that is why they understood the need for church unity: "We believe that no one should withdraw from the church, content to be solitary. The whole community must preserve and sustain the unity of the church, submitting to common instruction and to the yoke of Christ." They did not think that the church's oneness was simply an abstract principle, for they confessed that it is through the church that "pure doctrine can be maintained, vices can be corrected and suppressed, the poor and afflicted can be helped in their need, assemblies can be gathered in the name of God, and both great and small can be edified."[12] Perhaps modern enchantment with private spirituality can be challenged by an endangered church's confession of the necessity of Christian community. Perhaps American church proclivity to division can be challenged by a weak church's confession of the need for unity.

Reformed churches recognize the deep value found in receiving confessions of faith from other places and times, although they vary in the nature of the authority they grant to formal confessions. Among North American Reformed churches, the Presbyterian Church (U.S.A.) is precise in its acknowledgment of confessional authority. Its *Book of Confessions* contains eleven creeds, catechisms, and confessions from the early church (the Nicene Creed and Apostles' Creed), the Reformation era (the Scots Confession, Heidelberg Catechism, and the Second Helvetic Confession), the seventeenth century (the Westminster Confession and catechisms), and the twentieth century (the Theological Declaration of Barmen, Confession of 1967, and A Brief Statement of Faith). Both the Reformed Church in America and the Christian Reformed Church include in their confessional standards the Belgic Confession (1561), the Heidelberg Catechism (1563), and the Canons of the Synod of Dort (1619), as well as the Nicene Creed, the Apostles' Creed, and the Athanasian Creed from the early centuries of the church. All three churches are in the process of determining whether the Belhar Confession should be included among their confessional standards. The United Church of Christ does not specify formal confessional authority, declaring that it "receives the historic creeds and confessions of our ancestors as testimonies, but not tests of the faith."[13]

Reformed churches agree that the church's present witness is not confined to what we think and say in our own time and place. Affirming the convictions of those who have lived and died the faith before us is one form of the church's contemporary witness, together with the present witness of new statements of faith. From the Nicene Creed and Apostles' Creed to the formal confessions of present-day churches, the whole communion of saints bears witness to the grace of the Lord Jesus Christ, the love of God, and the communion of the Holy Spirit. Thus, contemporary confession of faith may find its full expression in the reappropriation of past articulations—not as accounts of what people used to believe, but as deep expressions of current faith and faithfulness.

Present witness is made not only in officially adopted confessions, but also in provisional accounts of faith that are intended for use in teaching and worship. While not part of the churches' formal confessional standards, the Reformed Church in America's "Our Song of Hope" (1978), the Christian Reformed Church's "Our World Belongs to God" (1986), and the Presbyterian Church (U.S.A.)'s "A Declaration of Faith" (1977) and "Presbyterian Catechisms" (1998) are significant expressions of Reformed confession making. In all of this, Reformed churches confess *the* faith, not inventive creations. Reformed confessing focuses on contextual continuity in the enduring faith of the Christian community, shaped by the grace of Christ, the love of God, and the communion of the Holy Spirit.

The Continuing Reform of the Church

Reformed confession of faith is not a casual undertaking. Churches typically make confession out of necessity, not simply because they think it would be a pleasant thing to do. Necessity comes in many forms, but most often churches are compelled to express their faith when they experience threats to the integrity of their witness coming from internal confusion about core matters of faith, from the culture's rival accounts of truth and morals, or from threats to the church's freedom.

Internal Confusion

Churches consistently express their faith when confronted by confusion about the truth of the gospel that jeopardizes the integrity of their proclamation. In the fourth-century Nicene Creed, the church confirmed fully Trinitarian faith in opposition to theologies that consigned Christ and the Spirit to subordinate status. The church's confession was more than ecclesial quibbling over a theological abstraction. The crucial question was whether God had come to humankind in the person of Jesus Christ or had remained aloof, only sending an emissary. The answer had profound implications for Christian confidence in the reality of salvation. Could Christians believe that Christ was "true God," and therefore trust that the salvation announced and accomplished in Jesus Christ was God's gracious will? Or was Christ something less than God, so that God's will remained mysterious—an uncertain purpose behind, above, and beyond the words and deeds of Jesus? In the seventeenth century, the Canons of Dort were adopted by a synod of the Reformed churches in the Netherlands to settle a great controversy concerning grace, election, and faith. Dort's formulations may seem overly scholastic now, but their intention was to confirm Christian confidence in the certainty of God's grace.

Culture's Challenge

Churches also express their faith to make clear to Christians the points at which cultural, social, and political realities embody norms and conventions that are contradictions of the gospel. In 1960s America, churches were faced with multiple forms of social fragmentation and antagonism. The United Presbyterian Church was convinced it had an insight into the gospel that needed to be heard by the world and by its own members. In its Confession of 1967 it declared, "God's reconciling work in Jesus Christ and the mission of reconciliation to which he has called his church are the heart of the gospel in any age. Our generation stands in peculiar need of reconciliation in Christ. Accordingly, this Confession of 1967 is built upon that theme."[14] The Reformed Church in America confessed Christian hope in the face of the culture's—and the church's—complicity in the social structures of sin. At the outset of "Our Song of Hope," the church confessed:

We know Christ to be our only hope.
We have enmeshed our world in a realm of sin,
    rebelled against God,
    accepted inhuman oppression of humanity,
    and even crucified God's son.
God's world has been trapped by our fall,
    governments entangled by human pride,
    and nature polluted by human greed.[15]

In the face of dominating social structures, the Christian Reformed Church declared:

As followers of Jesus Christ,
living in this world—
which some seek to control,
and others view with despair—
we declare with joy and trust:
Our world belongs to God![16]

Also in the twentieth century, the Presbyterian Church in the Republic of Korea adopted a new confession to make clear to a religiously plural nation what the church believes and why it engages in mission. In none of these confessions did the churches claim to be pure communities in a sinful culture; they recognized the need to make clear to themselves the Way of the gospel in distinction from "the way things are."

Threats to the Church

In 1930s Germany, the churches were faced with Nazi government pressure to compromise their theological and ecclesial independence. Representatives of Lutheran, Reformed, and United churches came together and spoke boldly:

Be not deceived by loose talk, as if we meant to oppose the unity of the German nation! Do not listen to the seducers who pervert our intentions . . . . We publicly declare before all evangelical churches in Germany that what they hold in common in this Confession is grievously imperiled, and with it the unity of the German Evangelical Church.[17]

The Theological Declaration of Barmen did not assume a protective or defensive stance, but rather set out six "evangelical truths" that proclaimed the church's freedom from all human events, powers, figures, and truths; and the church's freedom for the one Word of God, Jesus Christ.

Often, multiple motivations are present in churches' declarations of faith, but confessions that endure are more than bland restatements of Christian verities. A recent theological statement of the Presbyterian Church (U.S.A.) General Assembly may overstate the case, but it is true more often than not, "the church writes confessions of faith when it faces a situation of life or a situation of death so urgent that it cannot remain silent but must speak."[18] Since urgent situations are seldom unique to a particular time and place, the church may need to hear the voices of the whole communion of saints from all times and places. In this way, the integrity of confession can be protected from the distortions of ecclesial nearsightedness.

Confessional testing of the church's witness demonstrates the Reformed conviction that all confessions of faith must be interrogated by Scripture, which is the word of God to us and for us. C. Northcote Parkinson, a wry British observer of organizational life, makes a point about the business world that is also true of the church: "A diseased institution cannot reform itself. . . . The cure, whatever its nature, must come from outside."[19] The church does not and cannot reform itself. God reforms the church, judges the church's proclamation, and calls the church to renewed obedience and to continuing reformation.

Churches in the Reformed tradition understand themselves to be "reformed and always to be reformed (*ecclesia reformata semper reformanda*) according to the word of God (*secundum verbum Dei*)." This motto of the Reformed tradition makes clear that God has reformed the church, and that God will continue to reform the church. One popular but mistaken translation of the Latin motto is "the church reformed, always reforming," as if the church were always reforming itself, or worse, simply changing itself. Reform of the church is not mere change, certainly not "modernization," and never a product of the church's own achievement. The church is not the agent of its own reformation; reform of the church comes from the leading of God's word, made present in the power of the Spirit.

The church is always to be reformed "according to the word of God"—that is, in accord with, consistent with, the clear witness of Scripture. The Reformed tradition has always understood itself to be "Scripture-shaped." Twentieth-century Reformed theologian Karl Barth goes so far as to identify the *scriptural principle* as a primary characteristic of Reformed theology. "At their very beginnings the Reformed churches saw that truth is contained only in the word of God," says Barth, "that the word of God lay only in the Old and New Testaments, and that every *doctrine* must therefore be measured against an unchangeable and impassible standard discoverable in the Scriptures."[20]

Sixteenth-century Reformers were denounced for advocating change for its own sake. "We are accused of rash and impious innovation," wrote Calvin, "of having ventured to propose any change at all in the former state of the church."[21] Calvin responded that reform of the church's doctrine, worship, and governance had no ground other than "the exact standard of the Word of God." Reform of the church was happening because Christians "look for the good which they desire from none but God, that they confide in his power, trust in his goodness, depend on his truth, and turn to him with the whole heart, rest on him with full hope, and resort to him in necessity."[22]

Reform of the church, in the sixteenth century and the twenty-first century, grows from response to the gracious action of God; the church is always *to be reformed* by God. The Reformation began with a call to repentance, not a plan for change. The first of Martin Luther's Ninety-five Theses, posted on the door of the Wittenberg castle church in 1517, proposed that "when our Lord and Master, Jesus Christ, said 'Repent,' He called for the entire life of believers to be one of penitence."[23] The following ninety-four theses assert that the church does not control the shape of repentance or the terms of penitence. Instead, says Luther, the initiative lies with the Holy Spirit, the Scriptures, and "Christian doctrine." With ears that are open to hear, the church can listen for the Spirit's guidance in the Scriptures and in the church's tradition of "Christian doctrine."

Reformed understandings of Scripture and its use are not simple or uniform, but Scripture remains at the center of Reformed thought and life. The centrality of Scripture is more than a formal distinctive. Nothing less than the continuing reformation of the church is at stake in preserving ecclesial acknowledgment of Scripture's authority. Scripture is the primary means by which the Holy Spirit reveals God's truth and purpose to the church: "Reformed doctrine, in order to be itself at all, needs the free winds wherein the word of God is recognized in Scripture and Spirit; it needs the vastness and energy of untamed nature whereby once the Reformed churches, as by a volcanic eruption were 'born'—or, as Christian churches, born again. Reformed *by God's Word* is the ancient and real meaning of the name we bear."[24]

Calvin, Calvinism, and the Reformed Tradition

"Reformed" is the name we bear, not "Calvinist." Even so, it is appropriate to give sustained attention to Calvin, both historically and doctrinally. While he is not a privileged authority, a venerated figure to whom we must defer, Calvin's distinctive approach to Christian faith and life has influenced Reformed church life for centuries and is evident today in Reformed theology, worship, ethics, and polity. To understand who we are, it is always helpful to understand where we have come from. Together with Reformed churches throughout the world, we come from a long tradition that has its source in the Reformation stream fed by John Calvin.

We may not be particularly pleased to bear Calvin's legacy; *Calvinism* is not a happy word. It conjures up images of harsh judgments and unpleasant theological abstractions. Calvin himself is blamed for persecuting his opponents, policing the morals of individuals, and demanding strict adherence to a rigid theological system. He is accused of providing later generations with theological justifications for governmental tyranny and the abuses of capitalism. Scholars who explore the reality of sixteenth-century Geneva present a more favorable assessment. A recent Calvin biographer notes,

> The demonology of the past is in what may fervently be hoped to be terminal decline. The great stereotypes of the past, portraying Calvin as a bloodthirsty dictator and Calvinism as mindless moral rigorism, are—despite their occasional resuscitation in polemical writings—behind us.[25]

This may be too optimistic or too scholarly a judgment, for five hundred years after Calvin's birth, three popular yet misleading impressions of Calvin persist, even among Presbyterians and other Reformed Christians: a bleak doctrine of double predestination, the legalistic moralism of Geneva, and the burning of heretic Michael Servetus.

The reality of John Calvin is more complex than either his critics or his fans would have it. Like many major historical figures, he has been caricatured, making it difficult to appreciate his genius while remaining critical of his legacy. The difficulty is compounded because we do not have direct access to Calvin; we only have him together with centuries of his followers, his critics, and the ambiguous churches that developed under his influence. As another biographer puts it, "He was a man, and he became an ideology, a doctrine, almost a religion."[26] Churches of the Reformed tradition have rarely been slavish followers of Calvin, but they have found that his questions remain important and that his way of seeking answers continues to be helpful. As the primary initiator of the Reformed tradition, Calvin continues to be an important guide as we think and live the Christian faith.

Who was John Calvin? It may soften the caricature a bit to know that he was not Swiss, but French. Jean Cauvin was born at Noyon in 1509 and studied philosophy and law at universities in Paris, Orleans, and Bourges. While a student, Calvin experienced a "sudden conversion" to the truths of a growing movement that called for reform of the Catholic Church. This radical change led to a lifetime of devoted service to God and to the people of God. Forced to flee from France because of his reformist beliefs, he found refuge in Geneva, Switzerland's principal French-speaking city. The continuing persecution of reform-minded Christians in France was agonizing to Calvin. When he was only twenty-six years old, he wrote an appeal to the king of France, introducing a treatise he had written that systematically presented the position of Christians desiring reform. The *Institutes of the Christian Religion* was first published in 1536, then revised and enlarged several times by Calvin until its final edition in 1559. In addition to the *Institutes,* Calvin wrote commentaries on books of the Bible, a large number of essays and expositions, catechisms, letters, and hundreds of sermons. The standard collection of Calvin's writings fills fifty-nine volumes!

Calvin's leadership of the church in Geneva came about almost by accident and was always stormy. He sought to reform faith and faithfulness in the church, reinvigorating both its theological convictions and its moral action. His desire for reform was not limited to the church. Calvin had no interest in a theology abstracted from real life or confined to the church itself; he was convinced that Christian faith requires social responsibility and action. He wished to create an ecclesial community faithful to Christ, whose life of mutual love, forgiveness, and service would provide a model for the life of the civil society.

As a necessary outgrowth of his writing, preaching, and nurturing the life of the church in Geneva, Calvin worked tirelessly for a just social order. Refugee relief and resettlement, jobs for the unemployed, public education, and health care for all were among his concerns. He lashed out at dishonest business practices and public policies that ignored the needs of the poor. No matter seemed too small or too mundane. Calvin expressed deep interest in a more economical cooking stove for ordinary people and worked for a sanitary sewer system in the city. Calvin's zeal for reform sometimes led to excesses, but these should not negate his great insight: Faith and faithfulness are inseparable; theology and ethics are united. Not surprisingly, these convictions occasioned opposition both by those who disputed his theological views and by those who disagreed with his efforts to reform the church and Genevan society.

Calvin's combination of faith and faithfulness attracted people from all over Europe. They came to Geneva to see what was happening and to study the faith that led to such remarkable faithfulness. Scotland's John Knox called Calvin's Geneva "the purest school of Christ on earth." Those who spent time in Geneva later carried Calvin's thought home with them, spreading his theological insights and establishing Reformed churches throughout Europe. The Scottish reformation, spearheaded by Knox, became the greatest influence on American Presbyterianism, while reformation in the Netherlands, guided by Guy de Bray and consolidated by William of Orange, influenced America's Dutch Reformed churches.

Shortly after Calvin's death in 1564, his colleague and successor Theodore Beza wrote a laudatory biography. At the end of his account of Calvin's life, Beza wrote, "Since it has pleased God that Calvin should continue to speak to us through his writings, which are so scholarly and full of godliness, it is up to future generations to go on listening to him."[27] Future generations have continued to listen, not passively, but with a lively engagement that sometimes learns, sometimes argues, and sometimes discovers that contemporary questions and answers are revised by their contact with Calvin's questions and answers.

1. Marilynne Robinson, *Gilead* (New York: Picador, 2004), p. 114.
2. Arthur C. Cochrane, ed., *Reformed Confessions of the Sixteenth Century* (Louisville, KY: Westminster John Knox Press, 2003), p. 49.
3. Cochrane, *Reformed Confessions of the Sixteenth Century.*
4. Lukas Vischer, ed., *Reformed Witness Today: A Collection of Confessions and Statements of Faith Issued by Reformed Churches* (Geneva: World Alliance of Reformed Churches, 1982).
5. Philip Schaff, *Creeds of Christendom*, vol. 1 (New York: Harper & Bros., 1877), pp. 389ff.
6. Westminster Confession of Faith, XXXIII, *Book of Confessions*, Part I of *The Constitution of the Presbyterian Church (U.S.A.)* (Louisville, KY: Office of the General Assembly, Presbyterian Church [U.S.A.], 2007), 6.175, p. 158.
7. *Book of Order*, Part II of *The Constitution of the Presbyterian Church (U.S.A.)* (Louisville, KY: Office of the General Assembly, 2007), G-2.0100.
8. Confession of 1967, *Book of Confessions*, 9.02–9.03, p. 253.
9. Preface to "The Scottish Confession of Faith" in Cochrane, *A Collection of Confessions*, p. 165.
10. Confession of Belhar (1986), pcusa.org/theologyandworship/confession/belhar.pdf.
11. Presbyterian-Reformed Church in Cuba, "Confession of Faith," in Vischer, *Reformed Witness Today*, p. 172.
12. *The French Confession of 1559* (Louisville: Office of Theology and Worship, 1998), XXVI, p. 13, and XXIX, p. 14.
13. ucc.org/beliefs.
14. Confession of 1967, *Book of Confessions*, 9.06, p. 253.
15. Reformed Church in America, "Our Song of Hope," rca.org/Page.aspx?pid=313.
16. Christian Reformed Church of North America, "Our World Belongs to God," crcna.org/pages/our_world_main.cfm.
17. Theological Declaration of Barmen, *Book of Confessions*, 8.03, 8.07, pp. 247ff.
18. "Confessional Nature of the Church Report," in *Book of Confessions*, p. xiii.
19. C. Northcote Parkinson, *Parkinson's Law, and Other Studies in Administration* (New York: Ballantine Books, 1957), p. 110.
20. Karl Barth, "The Doctrinal Task of the Reformed Churches," in *The Word of God and the Word of Man*, trans. Douglas Horton (Boston: Pilgrim Press, 1928), pp. 240ff.
21. John Calvin, "The Necessity of Reforming the Church," in *Calvin: Theological Treatises*, ed. J. K. S. Reis (Philadelphia: Westminster, 1954), p. 184.
22. Ibid., p. 187.
23. Martin Luther, "The Ninety-five Theses," in *Martin Luther: Selections from His Writings*, ed. John Dillenberger (Garden City: Doubleday, 1961), p. 490.
24. Barth, "Doctrinal Task," p. 247.
25. Alister E. McGrath, *A Life of John Calvin* (Oxford: Blackwell, 1990), p. xiii.
26. Bernard Cottret, *Calvin: A Biography* (Grand Rapids: Eerdmans, 2000), p. 234.
27. Theodore Beza, *The Life of John Calvin* (Durham, UK: Evangelical Press, 1997), p. 140.

2

Why Tradition?

People are always shouting they want to create a better future. It's not true. The future is an apathetic void of no interest to anyone. The past is full of life, eager to irritate us, provoke and insult us, tempt us to destroy or repaint it. The only reason people want to be masters of the future is to change the past. They are fighting for access to the laboratories where photographs are retouched and biographies and histories re-written.

Milan Kundera, *The Book of Laughter and Forgetting*[1]

The Reformed tradition, confessions of faith, and John Calvin may seem remote from the realities of twenty-first-century North America. Adding to this difficulty, the concept of tradition itself is problematic, conjuring up images of a heavy past that weighs down progress by inhibiting insight and innovation. Especially in American culture, a widespread view that the past is a burden must be shed if we are to live freely in the here and now. Waves of immigrants to "the New World"— from the pilgrims who established Plymouth Colony to recent arrivals from Africa, Asia, and Latin America—have put their religious, political, or economic past behind them in search of a new life. The future, not the past, beckons Americans. In one of Gore Vidal's novels chronicling America's social and political history, a character observes, "The past for Americans is a separate universe with its own quaint laws and irrelevant perceptions."[2]

Disregard for tradition that pervades North American life is conspicuous even among Christians, many of whom believe that the dogmas of the past must be left behind if we are to live faithful lives in the present. Protestant Christians are especially disparaging of tradition. One hackneyed caricature of the difference between Catholics and Protestants is that Catholics grant inappropriate authority to tradition while Protestants look only to the Bible as the guide for Christian faith and life. Like most sweeping generalizations, this notion conceals more than it reveals; yet, it discloses the widespread belief that tradition distorts and obscures truth, and so must be swept away. Evangelical Protestants imagine that we must scrape off the doctrinal barnacles of centuries to return to the pristine Christian community of the New Testament, while liberal Protestants imagine that we must erase centuries of racism, patriarchy, and Eurocentrism to construct the pristine Christian community of a new era. Little wonder that we are unsure what to do with hundreds of years of Reformed history, not to mention the fifteen centuries of Christian faith and life that preceded the Reformation. Not surprisingly, we doubt the capacity of the Reformed tradition to help build shared faith and faithfulness among us.

Perhaps we should consider a historian's distinction between tradition and traditionalism: "Traditionalism is the dead faith of the living. Tradition is the living faith of the dead."[3] Traditionalism is an uncritical repetition of an accumulated past, while tradition is a lively conversation with those who have lived and died the faith before us. Traditionalism confines us to the musty archives of a lifeless past, but tradition opens up our place within the communion of saints, putting us together with sisters and brothers in the faith throughout time and space who have lived within the grace of the Lord Jesus Christ, the love of God, and the communion of the Holy Spirit. The experience and wisdom of our forebears in the faith are not inferior to our own; we do not stand at the apex of the history of God's Way in the world. The alternative to traditionalism, an unquestioning reception of the past, is not an unquestioning faith in the present. Rather, tradition flows from our past into our present as a life-giving stream.

Living Tradition

Wisdom about the nature of Christian faith and faithfulness does not begin with us, with our insights and actions. Canadian theologian Douglas John Hall notes: "By its nature Christian theology requires dialogue with and help from 'a usable past.' " Hall is not an antiquarian, simply enamored of earlier periods; he expresses theology's need for a *usable* past. "Theology," he writes, "unlike popular philosophies cannot be spun out of one's own or one's culture's immediate experience. It requires a tradition, a past, with which to struggle and from which to learn."[4] Hall's conviction notwithstanding, a danger looms over any age, surely evident in our own—arrogance toward those who have preceded us as we dispense with their lives and their wisdom in favor of our own experience and perceptions. The peril in turning from the past is particularly acute in the church, because we then ignore the rich heritage of Christian tradition that is a formative part of what makes us who we are as believers. The contemporary church is rooted in the beliefs and practices of the communities that preceded it. If we avoid serious conversation with the past, we are in jeopardy of accepting it mechanically or departing from it frivolously. Only if we engage the tradition thoughtfully can we both receive its fidelity to the gospel and critique its missteps.

It may be instructive to probe the church's deep tradition by listening to Irenaeus, a second-century bishop and theologian. Celebrated for his lengthy work *Against the Heresies*, a comprehensive refutation of mistaken speculations about the Christian faith, Irenaeus appealed to a summary of Christian belief known as the *regula fidei*, the "rule of faith." Rule of faith refers to the account of Christian faith and faithfulness given by early church bishops to new believers in preparation for their confession of the church's faith at baptism. As a basic digest of the Christian story, these summaries were the focal point of Christian identity for the church and for individual believers, setting forth distinctive Christian convictions and behaviors in the midst of an incompatible culture. "Rule" may be a somewhat misleading term, because the rule of faith was not promulgated by a central authority and its wording was not fixed. While the exact form of the rule of faith was specific to each bishop's diocese, the summaries were not divergent, for all expressed the central convictions that provided the whole church with norms of Christian faith and practice. Irenaeus himself sets out varying versions of the rule, but they were consistent with each other and with the accounts of other bishops. All followed the same three-part structure later developed in the Nicene Creed and Apostles' Creed. After almost nineteen centuries, we can recognize our faith in Irenaeus's version of the rule:

> And this is the drawing-up of our faith, the foundation of the building, and the consolidation of a way of life. God the Father, uncreated, beyond grasp, invisible, one God and maker of all; this is the first and foremost article of our faith. But the second article is the Word of God, the Son of God, Christ Jesus our Lord, who was shown forth by the prophets according to the design of prophesy and according to the manner in which the Father disposed; and through Him were made all things whatsoever. He also, in the end of times, for the recapitulation of all things, is become a man among men, visible and tangible, in order to abolish death and bring to light life, and bring about the communion of God and man. And the third article is the Holy Spirit, through whom the prophets prophesied and the patriarchs were taught about God and the just led in the path of justice, and who in the end of times has been poured forth in a new manner upon humanity over all the earth renewing man to God.[5]

The rule of faith expressed the gospel received from the apostolic witness, passed on through subsequent generations, and proclaimed in the church. It did not deal with every element of faith and it did not answer every question; it expressed the *core* of Christian faith, rehearsing the indispensable elements that make Christian faith what it is. A generation after Irenaeus, Tertullian followed his own rendition of the rule with the counsel that "provided the essence of the rule is not disturbed, you may seek and discuss as much as you like."[6]

Irenaeus, Tertullian, Athanasius, the Cappadocians, and others who struggled against false teaching drew the contrast between the church's enduring, commonly held tradition—the heart of Christian faith—and the unprecedented speculations of the heretics. One of Irenaeus's critical strategies was to mock the heretics for their disregard of the church's received tradition in their unseemly rush to outdo one another in devising something original and innovative. Irenaeus derisively notes, "Each one of them, as far as he is able, thinks up every day something more novel. . . . those of them who are acknowledged as the more modern endeavor to excogitate something new every day and to produce something that no one has ever thought of."[7] Irenaeus's reason for resisting novelties had nothing to do with a conservative fondness for stability, an antiquarian attraction to things from the past, or a fussy interest in scholastic precision. Irenaeus's concern was pastoral: He understood that knowing the truth about God and ourselves was vital if persons were to live fully within the good news of redemption. He knew that the corrosive effects of pagan culture could be resisted only through the reception of new life in the grace of the triune God. The rule of faith's defense against speculative innovation was, first, essential to the well-being of people. This pastoral purpose was made explicit in the Nicene Creed's formal articulation of the rule, where the truth of the gospel is framed by the declaration that it is all "for us and for our salvation . . . For our sake . . ."

Chronological Snobbery

Irenaeus confidently contrasted enduring truth with rash error, but we are less sure of our capacity to distinguish truth from heresy. Although we certainly do not wish to be counted among the heretics, we may make a somewhat more modest version of the heretics' mistake by turning our back on the seemingly tedious past as we search for something new, intriguing, and exhilarating. Our desire for originality even results in snubbing what was considered "new" in Christian thought and life bare decades ago. Perhaps we are guilty of what C. S. Lewis called "chronological snobbery, the uncritical acceptance of the intellectual climate common to our own age and the assumption that whatever has gone out of date is on that account discredited."[8] Twentieth-century theologians are now buried with those of previous centuries in the "history of doctrine" graveyard as we look eagerly for the latest proposal in "constructive" theology. Do we really imagine that the issues and problems we face are unique to our time and place? Do we truly believe that our thoughts and actions are at the pinnacle of human achievement, superior to all that has preceded us? Do we actually think that those who have lived and died the faith before us have nothing to tell us?

If we recognize the arrogance of ignoring the voices of our forebears, we may also realize that we have subjected ourselves to unseen limitations that diminish our capacity to know what is true. Our time is a period in time, just like all other eras; our place in history has horizons, just like all other locations. And so, like all places in all periods in time, we have a distinct outlook. We are able to see certain things quite clearly, but we are also blind to some things that people in other times and places saw in sharp focus. Lewis notes that

> We may be sure that the characteristic blindness of [our] century—the blindness about which posterity will ask, "But how *could* they have thought that?"—lies where we have never suspected it, and concerns something about which there is untroubled agreement.[9]

We may be able to detect the illusions of the past, but our own characteristic illusions go unnoticed, lurking in the shared assumptions we take for granted.

Contemporary Christians take for granted a wide range of convictions about God. We live in a culture, and a church, that assumes God's benevolence. We are certain that, like Mister Rogers, God likes us "just the way we are." We believe fervently that God is love—accepting, welcoming, hospitable, forgiving love. We are confident that God can be counted on to approve of us, for God understands that we try to be good people. When we slip up, God is always ready to forgive and to give us what we need to improve our lives. Our certainty that God loves us is reinforced by the hymns and praise songs we sing, the sermons we hear in church and on television, the popular media we enjoy, and the devotional literature we read. Confident of God's benevolent care, we are grateful that we have progressed beyond a remote, austere image of God, such as the one in the seventeenth-century Westminster Confession that describes God as "infinite in being and perfection, a most pure spirit, invisible, without body, parts, or passions, immutable, immense, eternal, incomprehensible, almighty; most wise, most holy, most free, most absolute, working all things according to the counsel of his own immutable and most righteous will."[10] Westminster's vision of God seems too severe; we much prefer to think of our God in the words of the late twentieth century's A Brief Statement of Faith:

> We trust in God,
>> whom Jesus called Abba, Father.
> In sovereign love, God created the world good
>> and makes everyone equally in God's image,
>>> male and female, of every race and people,
>> to live as one community.
> But we rebel against God; we hide from our Creator. . . .
> Yet God acts with justice and mercy to redeem creation.

In everlasting love,
> the God of Abraham and Sarah chose a covenant people
>> to bless all families of the earth.

Hearing their cry,
> God delivered the children of Israel
>> from the house of bondage.

Loving us still,
> God makes us heirs with Christ of the covenant.

Like a mother who will not forsake her nursing child,
like a father who runs to welcome the prodigal home,
> God is faithful still.[11]

When we hear the words of Westminster, we wonder, "How *could* they have thought that?" How could the "Westminster Divines" have painted such a somber picture of God? Didn't they know what we know about the everlasting love of God that will not forsake us, always welcomes us, and constantly develops our potential? Were they blind to the love of God? Actually, they were not blind, for the Westminster Confession of Faith does not stop with words about God's transcendent power. It goes on to affirm that God is "most loving, gracious, merciful, long-suffering, abundant in goodness and truth, forgiving iniquity, transgression, and sin; the rewarder of them that diligently seek him."[12] Although its seventeenth-century mode of expression is different from our preferred way of speaking, Westminster appears to give a fuller picture of God than does A Brief Statement of Faith. The Westminster Divines might well ask of us, "How *could* you think *only* that? Where in your articulation of God's love is there a clear sense of God's sovereign majesty, God's holy transcendence, God's eternal reign over all time and space? Have you no sense that God's love requires much of you and judges your departures from His ways of love? Where is your sense of holy awe?"

Questioned by Westminster, we may be able to hear more clearly the biblical witness that God is both loving and awe-inspiring, both forgiving and challenging. The psalmist understood: "I sing your love all my days, Lord, your faithfulness, from age to age. I know your love is unending, your fidelity outlasts the heavens" (Psalm 89:1-2) *and* "Great and dreaded God, you strike terror among the holy ones. Who is like you, Lord of might, clothed in truth, a God of power" (vv. 8-9). Paul understood: "I am convinced that neither death, nor life . . . nor anything else in all creation, will be able to separate us from the love of God" (Romans 8:38-39) *and* "How unsearchable are [God's] judgments and how inscrutable his ways" (11:33). Westminster may enable us to understand that the one who is "the Father of mercies and the God of all consolation" (2 Corinthians 1:3) will also require us to "appear before the judgment seat of Christ" (5:10). The point here is not that the Westminster Confession of Faith has it all right or that A Brief Statement of Faith is hopelessly inadequate. Both Westminster and A Brief Statement represent a particular context, and each contains particular insights that the other may not fully appreciate. We may say to Westminster that, while its articulation of God's love is technically true, its abstract language conceals the rich depth of the grace of the Lord Jesus Christ, the love of God, and the communion of the Holy Spirit that is captured in the more biblical language of A Brief Statement of Faith. We may also be able to thank Westminster for bringing to light our neglect of the scriptural witness to God's transcendent holiness. Without the awe of the Lord that is the beginning of wisdom, our understanding of God's love can easily become domesticated, reduced to a trivial expression of sentimental affection. While retaining the insight of A Brief Statement of Faith, we can open our ears to hear the voices of our forebears in faith, and thereby deepen our understanding of who God really is.

Voices Long Silenced

Tradition, the living faith of those who have gone before us, need not be a weight that must be shed to live free and faithful in Christ. Tradition can be liberating, freeing us from captivity to the limited perspective of our time and place. Without the capacity to transcend the taken-for-granted assumptions of twenty-first-century North America, we become prisoners in the tiny cell of "here and now." Ignoring the church's tradition because we fear that the past may oppress us only subjects us to the tyranny of the present. A Brief Statement of Faith calls upon the church "to hear the voices of peoples long silenced."[13] Among the long-silenced voices we need to hear are the voices of all who have gone before us in the living of Christian faith.

Attending to the Reformed tradition, we recognize that our forebears have something to say to us, and that we have something to learn from them. It provides us with conversation partners who can help us to ask questions that might not occur to us, and who can suggest answers that expand our possibilities. The Reformed tradition is not an authority to be accepted simply because it precedes us, or because we may be part of a denomination that claims its heritage. We do not substitute Calvin, or the confessions, or pronouncements of general assemblies and synods for the witness of the Scriptures. In fact, we measure their words by their fidelity to the Bible. Nevertheless, we listen to their words in the expectation that we will be guided, led, and instructed by their attempts to bear witness to the one Word of God, Jesus Christ.

Feminist theologians and scholars from racial ethnic communities within the church understand the necessity of probing the tradition. "If tradition is the still living and evolving past used to shape the future," says Letty Russell, "the question immediately arises, What if you do not have a past?"[14] The unpleasant reality is that the central role of women in the church and the vitality of racial ethnic communities of faith often have been ignored by the dominant tradition. Racial ethnic and women thinkers understand the dangers that come with the loss of their traditions and the need to reclaim what has been concealed. "Awareness of their own history and struggles is frequently nonexistent among women as a group," says Russell. "Yet it is toward such a search for a *usable history* that they must turn to build a still living and evolving past in order to shape their future as partners in society."[15] Gayraud Wilmore notes, "On the basis of the meaning of Black presence within the denomination and American Christianity as a whole, Black Presbyterians need to make a choice about whether they intend to carry on and enhance the tradition, or abandon it to the archives."[16] Recovering the pasts of women and racial ethnic communities (as well as recovering the reality of their suppression) is vital—not only for these groups, but for the enrichment of the whole church. There are times when enrichment comes in the form of rebuke that can lead to repentance of a deeply flawed past. South African theologian Allan Boesak reminds us that the evil system of apartheid was based on Christian principles! He lays bare the reality that "apartheid was born out of the Reformed tradition. . . . It is Reformed Christians who have split the church on the basis of race and color."[17] When A Brief Statement of Faith calls upon the church "to hear the voices of peoples long silenced," it also has in mind those who were consigned to the margins of the church's life. Among the long-silenced voices we are to hear are the voices of *all* who have gone before us in the life of Christian faith.

The Circle of Faith

Calvin was one of the principal leaders of the sixteenth-century Reformation, but he did not discard the entire life and faith of the church that had preceded him. Replying to the charge that Reformation teaching was a departure from church tradition, Calvin readily acknowledged that "the ancient fathers" (the tradition of the early centuries of the church) wrote "many wise and excellent things." But, Calvin continued, "so-called pious children of theirs . . . worship only the faults and errors of the fathers. The good things that these fathers have written they either do not notice, or misrepresent or pervert."[18] For Calvin, the Christian tradition contained both "faults and errors" and "good things." Throughout his own thinking of the faith, Calvin took notice of the tradition of the church, receiving from it many wise and excellent things. Calvin was also clear that even good things from the tradition were there "to serve us, not to lord it over us."[19]

Christian tradition—including John Calvin—must not lord it over us. Christian tradition—including John Calvin—can serve us. As we listen to the questions and insights and answers of our forebears, we hear questions we never thought to ask, insights we never imagined, and answers that never occurred to us. Our response to the questions, insights, and answers of our predecessors must be receptive, but also probing and evaluative. How else can we distinguish between "faults and errors" and "wise and excellent things"? Our critique of tradition is not based on our own presuppositions and perspectives, but on Scripture, which nourishes us as it nourished our forebears. Boesak was rightly critical of the faults and errors of the Reformed tradition, but he was also grateful for the tradition's good things. His indictment of the Reformed approval of apartheid was accompanied by his conviction that "in true Reformed theology . . . the recognition of the broken, sinful reality of our world becomes the impulse toward reformation and healing."[20]

What Jaroslav Pelikan calls traditionalism is marked by the compulsion "to give a re-statement to that great system which is known as the Reformed Faith or Calvinism, and to show that this is beyond all doubt the teaching of the Bible and of reason."[21] On the other hand, a truly Reformed understanding of the tradition is evidenced by Jeanne d'Albret, a sixteenth-century leader of the Reformed Church in France, who wrote to her cousin, the Cardinal d'Armagnac, "I follow Beza, Calvin, and others only in so far as they follow Scripture."[22] No element of the Christian tradition may simply be taken for granted. None should be appropriated just because it is ancient or venerable. Each must be assessed by the standard of the original, formative witness of Scripture. Like Jeanne d'Albret, we can appraise our forebears and our contemporaries by the standard of the Scriptures, following them as they are faithful to the biblical witness.

A naïve confidence in "progress" may have conditioned some of us to view the past as a series of deficient steps on the way to the pinnacle of modern wisdom. Elements of our inheritance even encourage this perspective. The Crusades, justifications of slavery, the Inquisition, denigration of women, and other errors are parts of the Christian tradition we wish to put behind us; we believe we have progressed beyond that. Others of us, in despair about the sad history of the church, may be tempted to leapfrog backward to a presumed golden age of the church, whether the New Testament era, the Reformation, or the 1950s. Neither romanticism about the present nor nostalgia for the past is true to historical and theological reality. Was the Spirit present and active in the early church, only to abandon succeeding generations of Christians to their own flawed devices? Did the Spirit sit on the sidelines of centuries of church life until becoming present and active in our time?

We stand in lively continuity with a living tradition. We cannot push our forebears aside as we stride back to the days of a pure church. Nor can we stand with our backs to our forebears, ignoring them as we press toward a more enlightened future. Rather, we sit in a circle with Ignatius and Athanasius, Gregory of Nyssa and Augustine, St. Francis and Luther, Calvin and Schleiermacher, Abraham Kuyper and Reinhold Niebuhr, Rachel Henderlite and Karl Barth, Edward Schillebeeckx and Leanne Van Dyk, along with countless anonymous disciples. Jesus Christ is at the center of our circle; our conversation with one another is about God with us, about the story of God's Way in the world. As contemporary members of the circle, we may speak scathing words to the corrupt Innocent VIII, quarrel with Calvin about predestination, and address skeptical questions to Barth. Yet we will also hear Luther rail against the Babylonian captivity of the church, be challenged by Schleiermacher's attempts to reach the "cultured despisers" of religion, face up to Calvin's appraisal of human sin, and wrestle with Elizabeth Johnson's proposals for language about God. As we sit in the circle of tradition, we are neither immodest judges nor submissive devotees. We are, with those who have gone before us, women and men who strive to know the way and the truth and the life, Jesus Christ, in whom "the fullness of God was pleased to dwell" (Colossians 1:19).

Not every Christian must study the history of the medieval church, master Calvin's *Institutes*, read Schleiermacher, or cope with Schillebeeckx (although some should, particularly ministers). The church's tradition is not limited to intellectual history, and scholarship is not our only means of access to the tradition. We stand within a Reformed tradition that has shaped

- our forms of ministry (ministers of Word and Sacrament, elders, and deacons);
- the way we govern our common life (consistories/sessions, classes/presbyteries, synods/conferences, and general synods/assemblies);
- our worship (the Genevan Psalter, the Westminster Directory for Worship, the *Book of Common Worship*); and
- the trajectory of our mission (Calvin, the Netherlands, Hudson River Dutch and New England Puritans, the Great Awakenings in America, the Confession of 1967).

Nothing in the history of the church's faith and life is the epitome of fidelity to the gospel, a pattern to be repeated endlessly. Yet the heritage of the church's faith and life must not be ignored, for it is the path by which we arrived at our present place. We are more likely to stay on the right paths if we know where we've been.

We smile at the witticism: The seven last words of the church are "We've never done it that way before." It's true enough that we get stuck in our ways (even when "the way it's always been done" was an innovation a mere fifteen years ago). Enthusiasm for new ways is not necessarily more faithful than reliance on old ways. Both the faith and life of past generations and new departures in faith and life must be subject to thoughtful critique, assessing the extent of their fidelity to God's Way as it has been revealed in Jesus Christ. Once we lay aside uncritical devotion to the old and uncritical enthusiasm for the new, we will discover that the promise of Jesus is sure: "I still have many things to say to you, but you cannot bear them now. When the Spirit of truth comes, he will guide you into all the truth" (John 16:12-13).

Teach Your Children Well

"Hear, O Israel: The LORD is our God, the LORD alone. You shall love the LORD your God with all your heart, and with all your soul, and with all your might. Keep these words that I am commanding you today in your heart. Recite them to your children and talk about them when you are at home and when you are away" (Deuteronomy 6:4-7). For Israel, and for the church, the Way of God is not an impersonal memory, but a living reality. How is this living reality kept alive in the community of faith? The presence of God, love for God, and fidelity to God's Way in the world are not self-evident truths that will be received and believed by everyone.

Our children are no more likely to incorporate our faith than they are to follow in our occupational footsteps or duplicate our political views. They do not believe precisely what we believe; they may not believe at all. In fact, that seems to be what has happened over the past fifty years. Sociological studies of mainline churches in general and the Presbyterian Church in particular demonstrate that much of the staggering membership losses during recent decades are the result of a steady exodus from the church of the church's children. For too many children of believers, baptism, Sunday school, and confirmation lead not to faithful discipleship within the body of Christ, but to effortless departure from the community of faith. One hundred years ago Christians sang confidently:

> We've a story to tell to the nations
> That shall turn their hearts to the right,
> A story of truth and mercy,
> A story of peace and light . . .[23]

Congregations that use newer hymnals no longer sing that hymn, perhaps because we are unsure that we have a story to tell to our children, let alone the nations. Or perhaps, against all evidence, we hope that the Christian story is self-evidently part of the fabric of American life and so will be absorbed by cultural osmosis.

Unless the community of faith has coherent convictions, shared beliefs, and common ways of being in the world, it will lack the identity necessary to differentiate it from the surrounding culture. The Christian community is not called to be a quaint religious ghetto in the midst of "secular humanism." Neither can the Christian community be content with communal and personal existence that is indistinguishable from the rest of the culture. "The culture" does not refer to opera, ballet, and art galleries, but is simply shorthand for customary social structures of meaning, ways of thinking and being that are integral to a society and its people.

Over a generation ago, H. Richard Niebuhr's *Christ and Culture* set forth the enduring Christian problem of the relationship between church and culture.[24] Is the church pitted against a hostile culture? At home in a friendly culture? Serenely transcendent over culture? Separated from culture as a distinct "kingdom"? Or is the church the transformer of culture? Niebuhr was convinced that the culture is not an evil to be avoided or a patron to be embraced, that the church does not live in the heights above culture or in a realm distinct from the culture. Niebuhr thought that culture, as part of God's good but fallen creation, is to be transformed, converted, and brought into closer coherence with God's Way in the world.

Yet, today, an increasing number of Christians suspect that the culture has transformed the church! Has the church bought wholesale the assumptions, approaches, and values of North American culture, losing touch with the distinctive beliefs and practices of Christian faith and life? The American church's accommodation to the culture is not as gross as Christian capitulation to Nazi ideology or as petty as dancing and card playing. It is more insidious, though, for we may not even notice that anything is at stake. As a church, and as members of the body of Christ, we simply accept "the way things are" without imagining that Christian faith gives us an alternative way of looking at the world.

For more than three decades, many American denominations have been preoccupied with interminable debates about two major moral issues, abortion and homosexuality. Poll results show that the views of Christians on these two issues mirror the views of the American population at large. There is little distinction between the range of Christian views and the span of opinion in American society generally, and the disagreements among Christians follow the lines of our society's differences. Furthermore, as the culture's views shift, so do the views of church members. Similarly, the church's concern for poverty, the environment, and race follow the culture's trajectories, with church discussion of these issues little more than mildly religious versions of social discourse. Does the Christian community have nothing to say about abortion and homosexuality that is different from the range of views within American culture? Do Christians have no distinctive contribution to offer on developing discussions about care for the earth?

The church/culture question is not confined to large social issues. Our culture's impact on the church may also be felt in easy Christian acquiescence to the norms of a consumer-oriented market economy. Are Christian congregations called to be full-service providers of religious goods and services? Should Christian denominations identify their market, brand themselves, and engage in media advertising? Do effective management models really define the shape of Christian ministry? The point is not to assert that there is *the* Christian position on large social issues, or that there is *one right* way to relate to broad social norms. It is only to suggest that when the Christian community has nothing to say that is different from the culture, no ways of living together that are different from the culture, it should not be surprised when its children abandon worship for Sundays at the mall.

Our tradition provides us with the wisdom of sisters and brothers who have preceded us in Christian living. Their convictions, forms of piety, and mission in the world cannot be adopted unchanged. Neither can they be ignored if we are to be faithful to the God who is Lord of all times and places. The Christian tradition, deep and wide, nourishes possibilities for faithfulness that will help us develop the knowledge of God and of ourselves that is true and sound wisdom for us and for our children.

1. Milan Kundera, *The Book of Laughter and Forgetting* (New York: Penguin, 1981), p. 22.
2. Gore Vidal, *The Golden Age* (New York: Vintage, 2000), p. 445.
3. Jaroslav Pelikan, *The Vindication of Tradition* (New Haven: Yale University Press, 1984), p. 65.
4. Douglas John Hall, *Bound and Free: A Theologian's Journey* (Minneapolis: Fortress, 2005), p. 73.
5. Irenaeus, *Proof of the Apostolic Preaching*, trans. Joseph P. Smith, *Ancient Christian Writers*, No. 16 (New York: Paulist Press, 1952), ¶3, p. 49.
6. Tertullian, "Prescriptions Against Heretics," in *Early Latin Theology*, ed. S. L. Greenslade (Philadelphia: Westminster, 1956), ¶14, p. 40.
7. Irenaeus, *Against the Heresies*, trans. Dominic J. Unger and John J. Dillon, *Ancient Christian Writers*, No. 55 (New York: Newman Press, 1992), I.18.1, p. 72; I.21.5, p. 80.
8. C. S. Lewis, *Surprised by Joy* (San Diego: Harcourt Brace Jovanovich, 1955), p. 207.
9. Lewis, introduction to *On the Incarnation*, by St. Athanasius (London: A. R. Mowbray, 1953), p. 5.
10. Westminster Confession of Faith, *Book of Confessions*, 6.011, p. 124.
11. A Brief Statement of Faith, *Book of Confessions*, 10.3, p. 267ff.
12. Westminster Confession of Faith, 6.011, p. 124.
13. A Brief Statement of Faith, 10.4, p. 268.
14. Letty M. Russell, *Human Liberation in a Feminist Perspective–A Theology* (Philadelphia: Westminster, 1974), p. 80.
15. Ibid., p. 81.
16. Wilmore, *Black and Presbyterian*, p. 90.
17. Boesak, *Black and Reformed*, p. 85ff.
18. Calvin, prefatory address to King Francis, in *Institutes of the Christian Religion* (Philadelphia: Westminster, 1960), ¶4, p. 18.
19. Ibid.
20. Boesak, *Black and Reformed*, p. 90.
21. Loraine Boettner, *The Reformed Doctrine of Predestination* (Grand Rapids: Eerdmans, 1932), p. 1.
22. Roland H. Bainton, *Women of the Reformation in France and England* (Minneapolis: Augsburg, 1973), p. 61.
23. "We've a Story to Tell to the Nations," *The Hymnbook* (Richmond, Philadelphia, New York, 1955), Hymn 504.
24. H. Richard Niebuhr, *Christ and Culture* (New York: Harper & Brothers, 1951).

3

Why Theology?

I have a secret shame: I always feel better—cleaner, revitalized—after reading theology, even poor theology, as it caresses and probes every crevice of the unknowable.

John Updike, *Roger's Version*[1]

The Reformed tradition has always been particularly attentive to serious, sustained thinking about the faith—theology. Thinking about Christian faith is more than theorizing about intellectual abstractions. Although there have been times in the church's life when theological thought has become overly speculative or pedantic, Reformed theology at its best has been grounded in the scriptural witness to God's Way among ordinary people in the real world. Truly Reformed thought has not been undertaken without the Bible or beyond the Bible, but rather has proceeded *from* Scripture and pointed *to* Scripture. Truly Reformed theology has not been undertaken apart from the reality of personal and social existence, but rather has been grounded *in* and addressed *to* human life.

John Calvin begins his *Institutes of the Christian Religion* by stating, "Nearly all the wisdom we possess, that is to say, true and sound wisdom, consists of two parts: the knowledge of God and ourselves."[2] Calvin was concerned with persons, families, and social structures, yet the common caricature portrays him as a relentlessly logical, systematic theologian, divorced from down-to-earth realities, producing volumes of dense conjecture. It is instructive to note that Calvin spent most of his time preaching and teaching the Scriptures as the best guide to understanding the truth about God and the truth about our lives. His monumental *Institutes of the Christian Religion* was composed not as a "systematic theology," but as a guide to the reading of Scripture. In his introduction to the final edition of the *Institutes*, Calvin wrote, "It has been my purpose in this labor to prepare and instruct candidates in sacred theology for the reading of the divine Word, in order that they may be able both to have easy access to it and to advance in it without stumbling."[3]

Calvin understood theology's purpose as bearing witness to the revelation of God in Scripture to deepen the life of faith and strengthen the life of discipleship. He was adamant that in the church's theological work "we are called to a knowledge of God: not that knowledge which, content with empty speculation, merely flits in the brain, but that which will be sound and fruitful if we duly perceive it, and if it takes root in the heart."[4] Unfortunately, Reformed Christians have not always followed Calvin's lead, and the tradition has seen its share of empty speculation. Perhaps that is why theology no longer enjoys a good reputation, even within the church.

Theology Scorned

Even though the Reformed tradition has valued ongoing theological work, particularly by ministers and elders, it sometimes seems that *theology* is a four-letter word—a curse, not a blessing. Political pundits use the word *theology* to refer to rigid ideological convictions. If a government official's views on defense policy, for instance, are held with unyielding tenacity, columnists write about the official's *theology*. Many Christians do not even notice this odd political use of the word because they also speak of theology in unflattering ways. *Theology* as often used in the church indicates abstract, overly intellectualized systems that are inaccessible to simple faith. Inside the church as well as outside it, *theology* has become a dirty word, an unpleasant term for arcane theories far removed from real life.

Perhaps our scorn of theology grows from an underlying despair. Endless disputes about theology have led to division, discord, and even wars. Clashing beliefs of the great world religions motivate books like Sam Harris's *The End of Faith*, Richard Dawkins's *The God Delusion*, and Christopher Hitchens's *God Is Not Great: How Religion Poisons Everything*. Christians themselves view with dismay the history of violence among churches, from the Thirty Years' War in the seventeenth century to the "troubles" in twentieth-century Northern Ireland. Even in the absence of religious violence, how can we take theology seriously when it appears to be little more than verbal wrangling about controversies that are never resolved? And how can we have confidence in theology when it seems to deal with unknowable realities?

Through all of this, the stereotypical theologian remains a lone scholar silently examining dusty tomes in a dimly lit library. Even when the picture is updated it remains an academic image—a single professor writing a book or delivering a lecture. These stereotypes of theology and theologians blend two unfortunate tendencies in the contemporary church: the assumption that faith is a private matter and the impression that serious thinking about the faith is a matter only for experts. These notions have regrettable consequences.

The assumption that faith is a private matter leads to faith that is oddly *impersonal*. Our lives are not lived alone, but together with other people, in families, friendships, and a range of social relations. Real life is interpersonal, shared life, and so faith that is kept to oneself soon becomes abstract, distant from common, everyday life. Privately held convictions and loyalties are concealed, suppressed, and inaccessible to others. When faith is confined to the interior lives of isolated individuals, it is little wonder that it means less and less to large segments of the population.

The assumption that serious thinking about faith is a matter for experts leads to theology that is *unqualified* for the task of seeking to know the truth about God and ourselves. Jesus Christ, who is Truth embodied, is not available only to those who are specially trained. When thinking about the faith is reserved for the "experts," their thought—indeed, most thought about the faith—becomes divorced from the life of the believing community, thereby losing the interest of the church as well as the world.

Is Theology Private?

American Christians live in a strange time for both the culture and the church. Faith—what we believe and how we live—is widely thought to be a private matter. In our society, politics and sex have been admitted to polite (and impolite) conversation, but religion remains taboo. People who talk openly about their faith are considered pushy, intruders into the private recesses of deeply personal convictions. Reticence about faith may be understandable in the broader culture, but talk about faith is carefully circumscribed, even within the *church*, where it is confined to worship and education! Even there we may assume that different people are entitled to diverse beliefs, that divergent views should not be pursued, and that no one's opinion should be challenged. Who are we to question another's beliefs? Even within the community of faith we think that each person's beliefs are inviolable; we do not want other believers to trespass on our private faith, and we avoid encroaching on theirs.

Our insistence upon private faith may reflect a lack of confidence in our own convictions about God and God's Way in the world. Frederick Buechner, a novelist and author of numerous books about Christian faith, provides us with a clever definition of theology:

> Theology is the study of God and his ways. For all we know, dung beetles may study man and his ways and call it humanology. If so, we would probably be more touched and amused than irritated. One hopes that God feels likewise.[5]

We smile as we recognize a measure of truth in Buechner's definition. God's ways are not our ways and God's thoughts are not our thoughts, so our words always fall short of the reality of God. God may be touched and amused by our feeble efforts at understanding, but we become irritated by unbending orthodoxies and bizarre speculation that masquerade as *the* truth that must be held to the exclusion of other insights. Yet, in spite of our reticence about faith, we are creatures who cannot avoid thinking and speaking. As we perceive the presence of God in our lives (or suffer a sense of God's absence), we think and speak about things that happen and how we understand them. Our words may not be adequate to express our experience, and they are surely not adequate to express the reality of God. Even so, unless we wish to confine God within our mindless silence, we do think and we do speak.

Since we do not keep our thoughts to ourselves, we sometimes speak with other people about our awareness of the presence of God and our questions about God's ways. How we interpret our experiences of God and our questions is seldom identical to theirs, but since it is the same God who is made known to us all, we have things to talk about. As we try to make sense of our own experience and as we try to understand the different experiences and insights of others, we may expand the conversation by inviting other people to join in the discussion. Sermons, Bible studies, mission planning meetings, worship, prayer groups, church school classes, and discussion groups are some of the ways in which the conversation is broadened. The conversation expands beyond face-to-face encounters as we sing hymns, say creeds, and read books that let us hear about the insights of people from other places and times who have also known the presence of God. We can share memory and hope with others as we try to understand God and God's Way among us.

All of this thinking and speaking is theology. It may be wise, insightful, and genuinely helpful, but like any thinking and speaking it may also be simpleminded, wrongheaded, unrealistic, or even dangerous. That is one reason theology cannot be a private matter, but must always be the shared activity of many people together. No one of us perceives the fullness of God's presence in the world. Each of us is confined to a particular place and time, with all the limitations that restriction entails. Moreover, no one of us is able to comprehend God's self-disclosure perfectly or to interpret God's will infallibly. It is as we remember together, hope together, and live together that we may be able to help one another remember more truthfully, hope more lovingly, and live more faithfully. The question, then, is not *whether* we will engage in theology; we do that every time we think about God, sing a hymn, pray, utter a religious cliché, study the Bible, or talk with a neighbor about church. The question is whether our theology will be casual or thoughtful, ignorant or informed, solitary or communal, faithless or faithful.

Faithful theology is intentional, sustained thinking and talking with others about God and God's Way in the world. It often begins with those close to us— family, friends, persons in our congregation and neighboring congregations. We talk about our faith and life at dinner tables, in church education groups, in hospital rooms, on mission trips, and at the movies. Our theological thinking is prompted by deeply personal joys and sorrows, by great national and world events, and by nagging questions that will not go away. Although this committed conversation may begin with those closest to us, it cannot remain there. Faithful theological discussion is wide-ranging, spanning geography and history, for God and God's ways are not confined to our own place and time. Books, the Internet and other media, and the ongoing tradition of the church enable us to have conversation partners from ancient Israel, first-century Corinth and Rome, and medieval Europe, as well as from modern Ghana, Korea, and Brazil. Men and women from other times and different places are partners in the discussion because they too wrestle with our questions and give answers that can inform our thinking and talking. Even if we are unaware of their part in the conversation, they affect us nonetheless, for they participate in the great dialogue of faith that reverberates throughout the church. If we listen to what they have to say, our thinking may be sharpened, our speaking may become more intelligible, and our acting may become more faithful.

Personal, Not Private

Habakkuk was an Israelite who lived seven centuries before Christ, during difficult times for the nation. He cried out boldly, challenging God to explain the sad state of the world. Why doesn't justice prevail? Why do the wicked prosper while righteous people suffer? Habakkuk's questions sound familiar, because they are our questions too. God answered Habakkuk, but the reply seemed obscure at best and evasive at worst. Habakkuk was not easily silenced, so he put the question to God again, vowing to wait with folded arms until he received a reasonable reply: "I will stand at my watchpost, and station myself on the rampart; I will keep watch to see what [God] will say to me, and what he will answer concerning my complaint" (Habakkuk 2:1).

There is another biblical story about a man who sat with folded arms because God's ways didn't make sense to him. When the Lord commissioned Jonah to go to the great and wicked city Nineveh, Jonah tried to avoid the mission God had given him. When he finally did what he was told, Jonah was disappointed to discover that the God-given message of judgment he preached resulted in evildoers' repentance and God's mercy. Jonah was interested in the punishment of the wicked, not in their redemption, and so Jonah became angry with the Lord for being "a gracious God and merciful, slow to anger, and abounding in steadfast love, and ready to relent from punishing" (Jonah 4:2).

Habakkuk's words and Jonah's story are voices in a conversation about God and God's ways. We are part of that discussion because we, too, wonder about the apparent absence of justice in the world, and we, too, may want God to punish the wicked. Habakkuk, Jonah, and all the other voices from the Bible are not lectures to be received passively, but invitations to dialogue in a common search for the truth. We may even be surprised to realize that God also joins the conversation with us. As God speaks with Habakkuk and Jonah we discover that we, too, are addressed. "There is still a vision for the appointed time," the Lord says to Habakkuk, "it speaks of the end, and does not lie. If it seems to tarry, wait for it; it will surely come" (Habakkuk 2:3). Is God's promise to Habakkuk a promise to us as well? Do these words of the Lord affect our response to the world's injustice? To Jonah, God addresses a simple question: "Should I not be concerned about Nineveh, that great city, in which there are more than a hundred and twenty thousand persons who do not know their right hand from their left, and also many animals?" (Jonah 4:11). Is God's question to Jonah a question to us as well? How might our answer affect our perception of wickedness in our world? What do we think about what we hear in Scripture? Do Habakkuk's and Jonah's words reflect our own perceptions? How do we respond to the Lord's words? What do we think and say and do about it all?

When the Bible becomes part of the conversation about faith and life, we are not simply leaping over the centuries to listen to single voices. The persons we encounter in the Bible are themselves part of a conversation within the community of faith in their time and place. Paul, surely one of the most prominent biblical voices, reminded the Corinthians: "I handed on to you as of first importance what I in turn had received" (1 Corinthians 15:3). Paul's thinking and speaking was not the musing of an isolated genius, but the wisdom of one who stood within the tradition of the gospel community. He received the Christian consensus, engaged in conversation with it, gained fresh insight, and passed it on to others. He expected them to be part of the ongoing conversation as well: "I speak as to sensible people; judge for yourselves what I say" (10:15). Throughout the history of the church, sensible people (and some not-so-sensible ones) have been judging for themselves what Paul and other biblical voices have to say. Their participation in the ongoing conversation has played a part in shaping the questions we ask and the answers we search for. No thinking and speaking about God and God's ways come to us untouched by the centuries-old conversation of the church, a conversation in which God continued to participate. The thinking and talking of the church throughout the centuries is not a hurdle to be overcome, but a heritage to be received with gratitude.

The church's tradition is not flawless. We may find it dangerously mistaken at points, and when we do we should argue with it strenuously. Our forebears in the faith took some wrong turns in their thinking about God and God's Way. Even the sharpest of those wrong turns (we call them heresies now), played a part in the conversation. As people listen to what others have to say they may disagree. When they do, they have to think through the reasons for their disagreement, presenting alternative possibilities. The history of the church is replete with instances of wrong turns that pointed out the right way.

Among the glaring mistakes within the Christian tradition has been the church's customary failure to include in the conversation people who are not white, Western males. Shortly before Jesus' death, a woman anointed him with expensive oil. When the disciples objected, Jesus said, "Truly I tell you, wherever the good news is proclaimed in the whole world, what she has done will be told in remembrance of her" (Mark 14:9). More often than not, the church's theology forgot her and the other women who followed Jesus, even as it neglected to include faithful women in its ongoing conversation. Women are becoming an integral part of the contemporary theological discussion, but others remain on the fringes. African Americans and Africans, Hispanic Americans and Latin Americans, Asian Americans and Asians, Native Americans, and others are too often confined to the sidelines of specialized scholarship, generally ignored by North America's white majority church when "real" theology is done.

In 1900, four-fifths of the world's Christians lived in Europe and North America. Today, two-thirds of the world's Christians live in Africa, Asia, and Latin America. Ghanaian theologian Kwame Bediako notes that "Christianity has become a non-Western religion; which means, not that Western Christianity has become irrelevant, but rather that Christianity may now be seen for what it truly is, a universal religion."[6] In 1900, leadership in American Reformed churches was overwhelmingly white and male, and the churches' ordered ministries were filled by men. Today, women exercise leadership throughout the life of the churches, and are increasingly prominent in ordained ministries. Although the membership of most Reformed churches remains predominantly white, persons of racial and ethnic diversity are progressively more present in positions of educational and ecclesial leadership. The theological voices of women, of racial ethnic communities, and of the global south can no longer be ignored. The theological conversation is becoming wider, deeper, and more faithful.

If we keep our beliefs to ourselves, it is little wonder that so many congregations are "gatherings of strangers." If we keep to ourselves what we think about God and God's Way in the world, and if we are in the dark about what others think, it should come as no surprise to discover that both personal faith and the faith of the community are impoverished. In concealing our own experience and closing ourselves to the experiences of others, we may become blind to the fullness of God's presence among us. God's Word is not addressed to an assortment of isolated individuals, but to human community. As we listen together, think together, and speak together, we may discover that "once you were not a people, but now you are God's people" (1 Peter 2:10).

Is Theology for Experts?

Even when we recognize that we think and talk about God and God's Way, and that we can do this together with other people, we hesitate to call this "theology." Theology seems to entail a level of knowledge and discipline that few church members have attained. Perhaps ministers are theologians, for they have spent years studying theology in graduate school. Yet even ministers hesitate to call themselves theologians. They think and talk about God and God's ways more than most church members, of course; it is their job, after all. Ministers know that they do not engage theological issues at the same level or with the same erudition that professors do. So, church members defer to ministers, who, in turn, defer to professors. While all of this may appear to be appropriate Christian modesty, it points to a real problem in the church. Theology has become an exclusively academic discipline, just like philosophy, sociology, or physics. It is thought to be beyond the ken of mere laypeople, or even of mere ministers. Although it is harmless—even wise—to leave chemistry to the chemists, it is a disaster to leave theology to the professional theologians.

Theology may be confined within the academy, but professors did not kidnap theology from ministers and members. It was handed over to them. Thinking and talking about God and God's ways is not a casual pastime; it requires attention to the resources of faith, the realities of the world, and the relationship between them. Not all theology professors are called to be ministers, but all ministers are called to be theologians. Professors can hardly be blamed for doing what all Christians are called to do but which many Christians neglect. Moreover, professors render a valuable service in and for the church. They think, speak, and write to help the church deepen its faith and broaden its faithfulness. If we sense that their thinking is sometimes distant from the lives of people in the believing community, we cannot place all the blame upon them. While academicians need to be in a conversation that involves the whole church, not just fellow professors, their work is often met by silence from congregations. Douglas John Hall complains that "there has been (to put it mildly) little demand for theologians within the various church structures . . . the churches have rarely given any conspicuous indication of being keen to have serious theologians in their midst."[7] Ministers and members go about the organizational business of the church, leaving serious thinking and speaking to the "real" theologians.

Theology is the calling of the whole church: professors, ministers, elders, deacons, and all members. Their roles are not identical. Ministers do not have to earn Ph.D.s and write books; members do not have to study Greek and Hebrew. Yet all are called to think and speak with each other about God and God's ways, contributing appropriately to the church's conversation. It is no more faithful for church members to neglect theology than for professors to absent themselves from worship. Ministers who abandon their theological vocation are no more admirable than members who fail to share their abilities, time, and money.

Theologians In and For the Church

Faithful thinking and talking about God and God's ways are particularly important for persons in positions of leadership in the church: pastors, elders, deacons, together with other teachers in the church. A glance at a few of the ordination questions for ordered ministries in the Presbyterian Church (U.S.A.)'s *Book of Order* reveals the Reformed tradition's conviction that ministers, elders, and deacons are to be thoughtful theologians in and for the church.[8]

> *Do you accept the Scriptures of the Old and New Testaments to be, by the Holy Spirit, the unique and authoritative witness to Jesus Christ in the Church universal, and God's Word to you?*

How can people make this vow unless they are engaged in reading, thinking, and talking about that witness and the Lord to whom it witnesses? The question requires more than mental assent to a theory of scriptural inspiration and authority. A faithful answer entails commitment to attentive reading, sustained study, and continual conversation within the community of faith.

> *Do you sincerely receive and adopt the essential tenets of the Reformed faith as expressed in the confessions of our church as authentic and reliable expositions of what Scripture leads us to believe and do, and will you be instructed and led by those confessions as you lead the people of God?*

Can people answer this complex question apart from sustained engagement with the Reformed tradition? The question requires far more than concurrence with the church's judgment that the confessions matter. Being instructed and led by the confessions assumes knowledge, understanding, and commitment that engage the knowledge, understanding, and commitment of others in the community of faith.

> *Do you promise to further the peace, unity, and purity of the church?*

Making this promise assumes more than casual assent to a string of ecclesial platitudes. Faithful response depends upon understanding historic Reformed perspectives on Christian peace, unity, and purity; thinking through the relationships among them; and joining with others to determine how they will be lived out within the community of faith.

Presbyterian sessions and Reformed consistories make many businesslike decisions about the life of the congregation, but it is the *primary* duty of elders "to strengthen and nurture the faith and life of the congregation committed to their charge."[9] Elders have a special responsibility to think and talk together about Christian faith, equipping themselves to help the whole congregation think through its faith, so that congregational life will be marked by faithful discipleship. As deacons exercise their ministry of "sympathy, witness, and service after the example of Jesus Christ,"[10] they are called to think theologically about the Lord and Savior to encourage faithful congregational discipleship. Ministers of the Word and Sacrament are expected to do many things (too many things?), but primary among them is the responsibility for "studying, teaching, and preaching the Word."[11] All who "teach" in the church are called to be "sound in the faith," so that the community of faith will live faithfully.[12]

Why bother with theology? Why should elders, deacons, teachers, and all members study, think, and discuss theology? It is not because Reformed Christians are intellectual, dogmatic, or impractical. Rather, what we think and say shapes who we are and how we live. What we believe forms how we act. It is a historic conviction of the Presbyterian Church that

> There is an inseparable connection between faith and practice, truth and duty. Otherwise, it would be of no consequence either to discover truth or to embrace it.[13]

Only if the way we live does not matter can we dismiss theology as of no consequence. Theology seeks to discover truth and embrace it so that our lives might be lived in faithfulness to God and love for all people.

The Theological Vocation of Pastors

Theology is the calling of the whole church, but in these times in North America pastors need to recover their theological vocation—not for their own sake, but for the sake of church members and for the sake of all those who have nothing to do with the church, or even with Christian faith. Marilynne Robinson, winner of both the Pulitzer Prize for fiction and the Grawemeyer Award in religion for her novel *Gilead*, has little patience for ministers who neglect their theological vocation. She understands that pastors do not want to appear pretentious, talking over the heads of parishioners, but she insists that just as doctors should know medicine, ministers should know theology. "That's what they're there for," Robinson says. "The idea that in their sermons pastors have to speak to people in almost infantile terms about things that they can read in the daily newspaper is an insult to others who are there to hear something that they do not know."[14]

Theologian Karl Barth and novelist Marilynne Robinson share the same concern. Eighty years before Robinson's interview, Barth addressed a pastors' conference in Germany. He described to his audience of pastors what is in the hearts of church members as they make their way to worship on Sunday morning. They come, said Barth, with a great expectancy, a great hope that there will be an answer to their fundamental, yet generally unspoken, question: *Is it true?* "Is it true, this talk of a loving and good God, who is more than one of the friendly idols whose rise is so easy to account for, and whose dominion is so brief? What the people want to find out," said Barth, "is, *Is it True? . . .* they do not want to hear mere assertions and asseverations, however fervent and enthusiastic they may be. They want to find out and thoroughly understand the answer to this one question, *Is it True?*"[15] If ministers are to be at all useful in the asking and answering of this seldom-voiced but often-thought question, they must engage in serious, sustained thinking about Christian faith and life. *Is it true?* The question is not theoretical, for the shape of questioners' lives depends on the answer. The capacity of ministers to be useful to questioners in answering the question beneath all questions depends upon their commitment to read, talk, study, and learn Christian theology.

Critique and Reform

At the beginning of his massive, multivolume *Church Dogmatics*, Karl Barth declares that theology is the church's "self-test." The church engages in theological thinking to put to itself the question of the truth of its proclamation and its action. "The question of truth, with which theology is throughout concerned," says Barth, "is the question as to the agreement between the language about God peculiar to the Church and the essence of the Church . . . which is Jesus Christ."[16] A primary task of theology is critical thinking about what the church says and does. It is a primary task because it has to do with the truth about God, and about us, and about God's Way among us in the world. Theology's critical task is not confined to secluded inner-church matters and is not limited to cool and detached investigation. Kristine Culp, inspired by the call of the eighteenth-century French Calvinist Marie Durand—*Résister*—recognizes that theology is a call to engagement. "At its best," she says, "Reformed thought offers a *call* to resist idolatry with confessional and social-cultural-political engagement . . . It poses 'a very great question' and struggles to answer it in every age and situation."[17]

Theology is not an ecclesial public relations endeavor, but the church's critical assessment of its own life, a critique of its speech and its actions. Theology's task is to address the fidelity of the church's life in the world before addressing the life of the world. Theology calls into question idolatries within the church before it bemoans the idolatries of the culture. Theology, far from being an abstraction that has little to do with the real life of congregations and their members, is the church's means of maintaining honesty about itself. Whenever theology abandons its task of critique it deteriorates into a churchly ideology that seeks only institutional success. On the other hand, whenever theology abandons its task of building up the body of Christ it is reduced to intellectual speculation that seeks only academic or popular approval. Thinking the faith in serious, sustained conversation within the church is an essential aspect of loving the Lord our God with all our heart, soul, *mind*, and strength, so that we can love our neighbors as ourselves.

The church finds itself in a strange place these days, preoccupied with issues of declining membership and loss of institutional attractiveness. In such times, it is tempting to look for answers in more effective management or more appealing programs. Yet the heart of church life is not its organization or its activities, but its faith and faithfulness.

> . . . thought-less faith, which has always been a contradiction in terms, is today a stage on the road to the extinction, not only of Christianity itself, but of whatever the architects of our civilization meant by 'Humanity.' Only a thinking faith can survive. Only a thinking faith can help *the world* survive!"[18]

Does that sound too dramatic? Perhaps. Yet even the most successful church programs are empty shells if they do not express the good news of new life in Christ. Churches are not called to be one more community organization providing attractive services to fill the discretionary time of middle-class Americans. Churches are called to live a new way—God's Way—in the world. Theology has something to do with the discovery, understanding, and living of that Way.

The young Karl Barth spoke of the church's disparagement of theology as a great perplexity. Why does the church so often disregard earnest, shared consideration of God and God's new Way in the world? Barth proposes a depressing possibility.

> *Had* we something more essential and authoritative to say, *had* we a theology convincing to, and accepted by, definite and increasing groups of people, *had* we a gospel which we *had* to preach, we should think differently. On the whole we do not have such a gospel in our churches. . . . The question of right doctrine introduces us to the vacuum *inside* our churches.[19]

Our neglect of theology may be a symptom of ecclesial anemia, a sign of our diminished capacity to seek the truth about God and ourselves with moral courage and intellectual rigor. If so, the call to theological engagement is far more than a call to thought; it is a call to renewed life.

What does the church have to say that no one else can say? This is "the very great question" that shapes the subtitle and theme of John Leith's book, *The Reformed Imperative.*[20] The answer to the question is not self-evident. The answer comes through faithful engagement with the scriptural witness to God's self-revelation, discerning engagement with contemporary culture, and sustained thinking and talking about God's Way in the world. Only when the church attends to its theological calling will it know what to say and discern how to say it. The world has little interest in a church that proclaims a vaguely religious version of what a profusion of ideologies, institutions, and images have to say. Yet those ideologies, institutions, and images devote far more effort to attaining clarity about both message and audience than does the church. Theology is not an ecclesial luxury; theology is necessary to the credibility of the church's witness and the fidelity of its mission.

Novelist, playwright, and scholar Dorothy Sayers's observation about mid-twentieth-century England appears to be equally true of contemporary North America:

> It would not perhaps be altogether surprising if, in this nominally Christian country, where the Creeds are daily recited, there were a number of people who knew all about Christian doctrine and disliked it. It is more startling to discover how many people there are who heartily dislike and despise Christianity without having the faintest notion what it is.[21]

Theology—thinking the faith—is the task of knowing "what it is." Knowing the faithful shape of Christian belief is not the end itself, but the means to expand our praise of God, deepen our devotion to Christ, and conform our proclamation of the gospel to the witness of the Holy Spirit. Only then will we have something to say to the gospel's "cultured despisers," its disinterested passersby, and its curious onlookers.

1. John Updike, *Roger's Version* (New York: Alfred A. Knopf, 1986), p. 41.
2. Calvin, *Institutes*, 1.1.1., p. 35.
3. "John Calvin to the Reader," *Institutes*, p. 4.
4. *Institutes*, 1.5.9., p. 61.
5. Frederick Buechner, *Wishful Thinking: A Theological ABC* (New York: Harper & Row, 1973), p. 91.
6. Kwame Bediako, *Jesus and the Gospel in Africa* (Maryknoll, NY: Orbis, 2004), p. 3.
7. Hall, *Bound and Free*, p. 7.
8. *Book of Order*, W-4.4003.
9. *Book of Order*, G-6.0304.
10. Ibid., G-6.0401.
11. Ibid., G-6.0202.
12. Ibid., G-1.0305.
13. Ibid., G-1.0304.
14. Debra Bendis, "A Pastoral Voice: An Interview with Marilynne Robinson," *The Christian Century* 123, no. 7 (April 4, 2006).
15. Barth, "The Need and Promise of Christian Preaching," in *The Word of God and the Word of Man*, trans. Douglas Horton (Pilgrim Press, 1928), p. 108.
16. Barth, *Church Dogmatics*, I.1., p. 3.
17. Kristine A. Culp, "Always Reforming, Always Resisting," in *Feminist and Womanist Essays in Reformed Dogmatics*, ed. Amy Plantinga Pauw and Serene Jones (Louisville: Westminster John Knox Press, 2006), p. 158.
18. Hall, *Thinking the Faith* (Minneapolis: Fortress Press, 1989), p. 13.
19. Barth, "Doctrinal Task," p. 221.
20. John Leith, *The Reformed Imperative: What the Church Has to Say That No One Else Can Say* (Philadelphia: Westminster Press, 1988).
21. Dorothy Sayers, *Creed or Chaos?* (Manchester, NH: Sophia Institute Press, 1949/1974), p. 20.

4

One Holy Catholic
and Apostolic Church

Are you a Christian?
   No, I'm not a Christian.
What do you believe, then?
   Believe about what?
The things that religious people think are important. Whether there is a God. How do you
explain evil? What happens when we die? Why are we here? How ought we to live our lives?
                                       P. D. James, *The Children of Men*[1]

The North American landscape is peppered with churches: Reformed and
Methodist, Roman Catholic and Lutheran, Greek Orthodox and Pentecostal,
Episcopalian and Baptist. Throughout the world, more than two billion Christians
are dispersed in thousands of separate, sometimes antagonistic church bodies. The
Yearbook of American and Canadian Churches lists hundreds of distinct denominations
in the United States and Canada alone.[2] Moreover, in what some have called a
postdenominational era, independent churches seem to multiply as rapidly as fast-
food restaurants. Even among churches that claim a common heritage, separation
is evident. The Reformed family represents only one ecclesial tradition, yet within
the United States there are forty-five Reformed denominations, twenty-one of
them Presbyterian! The worldwide Reformed family numbers more than seven
hundred distinct bodies, ranging from the Reformed Church of East Africa,
through Eglise Réformée de France, Igreja Presbiteriana do Brasil, the Church
of Scotland, Presbyterian Church of Korea (TongHap), the Uniting Reformed
Church in Southern Africa, and Karo Batak Protestant Church in Indonesia.[3]

Yet all of these traditions and denominations are *Christian* churches. Beyond
all-too-apparent separation and competition, an underlying unity—a recognizable
connection—binds communities of Christian faith together. This bond is stronger
than the loose ties of historical accident, organizational structure, or sentimental
attachment. It is a link forged from certain core beliefs. Beneath the real differences
are shared convictions linking Reformed churches in the United States, Catholics
in Italy, Pentecostals in Brazil, Orthodox in Russia, and millions of other Christian
bodies in this country and throughout the world. Churches of the Reformed tradition
share fully in this underlying unity of faith, the recognizable pattern of beliefs and

practices that forms Christian communities. The reality of distinctive Reformed perspectives does not obscure essential unity with the faith of the church catholic.

It may seem self-evident to begin exploring common faith by saying that all Christians believe in God. According to opinion polls, so do more than 90 percent of all Americans, including Jews, Muslims, and adherents of other religious faiths, as well as individuals with no connection to any religious community. Casual talk about belief in God (or atheism, for that matter) does not say much, and may be misleading. As a young priest, British New Testament scholar and bishop N. T. Wright served as a chaplain at Worcester College, Oxford. His welcoming visits to first-year students were often marked by their comment, "You won't be seeing much of me; you see, I don't believe in God." Wright developed a standard response: "Oh, that's interesting; which god is it you don't believe in?" The students were always surprised because they regarded the word *God* as having one self-evident meaning. Often, after students stumbled through a few characteristics of the god they didn't believe in, Wright would comment, "Well, I'm not surprised you don't believe in that god. I don't believe in that god either."[4]

Christian beliefs about God are distinct, differing in important respects from the beliefs about god in generic religiosity and in other living faiths. The question is whether Christian beliefs about God have any greater claim to truth than the convictions of other religious traditions. Do all religions fumble about in search of an essentially unknowable divinity? Are all religions nothing more than cultural variations? Is religious faith merely an accident of birth or a matter of personal preference? These questions are important, but they may begin at the wrong point, for the underlying question concerns the truth about God: Who is God, *really*?

It is clear enough that the distinctive beliefs of various religious faiths are not inconsequential. Beliefs express our understanding of whom we worship, who we worship focuses how we see the world, and how we understand the world guides how we live. On the surface, it may seem to make sense to say that all religious people, of whatever faith, worship the same God. On another deeper level, it matters a great deal how people conceive of the god(s) they worship. It matters, first, because God is who God is. No one possesses the absolute and complete truth about God and God's Way in the world, but that does not mean that we are reduced to hollow speculation and arbitrary opinions. God is who God is, and so what people believe about God may be either closer to or farther from the reality of God's being. Is God gracious to all people or does God demand obedience as a condition for love? Does God have a purpose for human life or are we subject to impersonal fate? Is God close to us, caring about us and for us, or is God remote and unconcerned? Can we bargain with God or does God deal justly with all? Surely, these and other questions, and the answers we give, make a difference that goes beyond diverse religious approaches or varieties of worship. Who we believe

God to be shapes how we understand the world, what we value, and the way we live our lives.

These questions take on added significance as North America undergoes a rapid transformation into a religiously plural society. Hindus, Buddhists, and Muslims are no longer an exotic presence on the pages of *National Geographic*. They are our neighbors, co-workers, and friends. For most of our nation's history, Christianity was the assumed religious expression of most Americans. No longer. As tens of thousands, now millions, of new immigrants bring their religious faiths with them to America, they meet a Christianity that has accommodated itself to its culture and is no longer certain of its own truth. Christians and their churches are ill prepared to deal *theologically* with the profusion of mosques, temples, and faithful adherents of other faiths. Religious pluralism and the church's theological response are complicated matters that require the church's sustained attention; it may be the most critical theological matter before the church. However, addressing religious pluralism begins at a more basic level: exploring *Christian* belief in God.[5]

Emmanuel—God with Us

All Christians believe in God, and while Christians differ on many important theological and ethical issues, we share certain core convictions about God. Preeminent among these shared convictions is the belief that God has most fully shown us who God is in the birth, life, death, and resurrection of Jesus Christ. "No one has ever seen God," says the Gospel according to John. "It is God the only Son, who is close to the Father's heart, who has made him known" (John 1:18). Christians believe that God is not a generic deity or a remote, unknowable mystery, for God has chosen to become known in human terms, in a human life, in Jesus of Nazareth. Growing out of this basic conviction is the insight that we experience the presence of the one God in three interrelated ways: as Father, Son, and Holy Spirit—the Trinity.

John Calvin shaped his theology around two related issues: the knowledge of God and of ourselves. What can we know about God, what can we know about ourselves, and what is the connection between the two? Calvin understood that our knowledge of God is not an intellectual accomplishment, but rather the result of God's self-disclosure. We do not discover God; God makes himself known to us. Human speculation about God cannot arrive at true knowledge of God; our desires and anxieties, our projections and insensitivities will always result in a god of our own imagining. We do not have to speculate or make guesses about God. We are human, subject to the limitations of human thought, but God does not abandon us in our limitations. Calvin says that God "accommodates" human understanding by revealing his very Being to us in ways we can comprehend: "For because our weakness does not attain to [God's] exalted state, the description of it must be accommodated to our capacity so that we may understand it."[6] God's accommodation to our limitation goes beyond making himself known to intellectual comprehension. Because it is impossible for human understanding to grasp the fullness of God, God becomes accessible to human understanding by becoming present to us in human terms, in a human life, in Jesus of Nazareth.

In a characteristically delightful image, Calvin says that God speaks "baby talk" to us. Calvin asks if we can imagine,

> As nurses commonly do with infants, God is wont in a measure to "lisp" in speaking to us? Thus such forms of speaking do not so much express clearly what God is like as accommodate the knowledge of him to our slight capacity.[7]

We cannot imagine God. We do not have to *imagine*, because God has made himself known to us in a way we can comprehend. God's accommodating use of "baby talk" is an expression of love for humankind that leads God to relate to us lovingly, in ways we can understand.

The earliest Christians affirmed that God has spoken to us most revealingly in Jesus of Nazareth: "Long ago God spoke to our ancestors in many and various ways by the prophets, but in these last days he has spoken to us by a Son" (Hebrews 1:1-2). God spoke with more than words; God spoke in the fullness of a human life: "The Word became flesh and lived among us" (John 1:14). This Jesus was a real human being, not merely God disguised in human clothing. Yet Jesus was not only a human being, for God was truly present in him. The church joyfully declares that Jesus Christ "is perfect both in deity and also in human-ness; this selfsame one is actually God and actually human."[8] The human being, Jesus of Nazareth, is also Emmanuel, God with us. The theological term is *incarnation*, becoming flesh. Beneath the sentimentality and commercialism of "the holidays," Christmas is our continuing celebration of the astounding reality that God has accommodated himself to us, becoming known to us and accessible to us in the way we can best understand . . . in the terms of a human life.

Once we fathom the marvelous news that God has become one with us in Jesus of Nazareth, we begin to perceive that incarnation is not confined to the moment of birth in a Bethlehem stable, but encompasses Jesus' whole life. Then the life and teachings of Jesus become significant to us in a new and fuller way. If God was truly present in the life of Jesus, then Jesus was far more than the founder of a great religion (like Mohammed) and far more than an enduring moral teacher (like Socrates). *God* was in Christ, and so Jesus' words and actions reveal uniquely who God is, showing God's Way in the world. "God is love," we say, and so God is. This definition avoids abstraction because we see and hear God's love in human terms, in the life of Jesus.

Jesus was notorious for the company he kept. "Why does he eat with tax collectors and sinners?" people asked (Mark 2:16). Why indeed? His odd behavior only led people to cry out, "Look, a glutton and a drunkard, a friend of tax collectors and sinners!" (Luke 7:34). As we see Jesus' intimate fellowship broaden beyond disciples to include strangers, undesirables, Pharisees, immoral people, outcasts, and foreigners, we begin to comprehend the specific reality of God's love. Jesus opened himself to people who were shut out by the society of his day: women, foreigners, children, sick people, crooks, and collaborators. Can we see in the life of Jesus that God is open to all people, not just to "worthy" people? Can we realize that God's love does not depend upon human deserving? If we can, we may begin to recognize that *we* are among those who are the friends of Jesus. Our own inadequacies, failures, and cruelties do not separate us from the love of God in Christ Jesus. We do not have to be successful, powerful, or pious to be loved by God. That is *good news*, the *gospel*.

Knowing the reality of God's love through Jesus' life rescues us from sentimental notions of divine love that reduce God to a doting grandparent who forgives everyone everything. Jesus' hospitality did not lead to casual conversation with tax collectors about revenue collection techniques or joking with sinners about people who took religion too seriously. Jesus called all people to radical change in belief and practice. In Jesus we see the love of God embracing people who are "outside the camp," but we also see God's love inviting people into a new life within a new camp. God's love calls for repentance, for turning from old ways and beginning to live God's Way. "Those who are well have no need of a physician, but those who are sick," Jesus said. "I have come to call not the righteous but sinners" (Matthew 9:12-13). Emmanuel, God with us, came to *heal* sinners, to call them to *new* life.

We also see who God is in what Jesus said. Most of us are familiar with parables such as the Prodigal Son and the Good Samaritan, and sayings such as "love your enemies" and "do to others as you would have them do to you." We may be *too* familiar with them, missing the startling things they say about God's Way in the world. Jesus' teachings are more than mere moralisms or tips for living; they reveal who God is, who we can be, and what life can become within God's Way.

Jesus' parables are often understood as real-life stories told to make a particular theological or ethical point. In these stories, we encounter familiar figures such as laborers, bosses, judges, farmers, and shepherds, and find ourselves in everyday situations of loss and joy, hypocrisy and faithfulness, prudence and recklessness. Even though the sociological specifics are distant from contemporary American life, the parables relate understandable situations and familiar figures. On closer examination, we begin to notice that discordant elements usually appear in the midst of the parables' everydayness. "Suppose one of you has a hundred sheep and loses one of them—what do you do? . . . Or suppose a woman who has ten silver coins loses one of them—what does she do?" (Luke 15:4, 8; TEV). Against all efforts to make Jesus' subsequent answers sensible, the behaviors of the shepherd and the woman are odd indeed. The shepherd abandons ninety-nine sheep to search for one, jeopardizing the flock with no guarantee that the one will be found. Like us, the woman who lost a coin might spend a bit of time looking for it. However, to spend all day looking, turning the house upside down until the coin is found, and then throwing a block party to celebrate her success? The parables do not tell us stories about the way the world is; they narrate a way of looking at the world that turns the expected on its head. The peculiar element in the stories causes us to turn away from the way things are toward the way things might be.

What is the kingdom of God like? Jesus told stories about a man who planted a mustard seed in his garden and watched it grow into a tree providing shelter for the birds, and a woman who mixed yeast into a huge quantity of flour. These may appear to be stories of small beginnings and dramatic results, until we know what Jesus' original hearers surely knew. Mustard seeds grow into shrubs, not trees, and garden shrubs are not suitable nesting places for birds. Only unleavened bread was suitable for feasts in Israel, and so a good Jewish woman would not put yeast into a celebration-sized quantity of dough. Jesus' parables do not relate ordinary behavior to present us with obvious lessons. Instead, they call into question our assumptions about the way the world works, and open a new horizon of possibilities that orients us to God's new Way in the world.

We often try to make Jesus' teaching fit into our ways of thinking, but the otherness will not go away. Anyone with ears to hear recognizes that his sayings abound with denials of common sense:

> the first will be last and the last first . . .
> love your enemies . . .
> whoever wants to be great must become a servant . . .
> when you're forced to do something, do it a second time willingly . . .
> no more tit for tat . . .
> you have heard it said, but I say to you.

These are not isolated instances of quirky folk wisdom, meant to be buried under a thousand qualifications. They are evidence of God's profound reversal of "the way things are," God's refusal to let the tired old way of the world be the last word in a tragic tale. The word of the Lord came to the prophet Hosea—"I am God and not a man, the Holy One in your midst" (Hosea 11:9, ESV). In Jesus, the Word made flesh, we see and hear God's Way, not the all-too-human course of the everyday.

The Jesus we encounter in the Gospels calls for our response. Will we remain in the taken-for-granted course of ordinary life, or will we turn toward the unexpectedly new possibilities that he opens for us? What Jesus did and said is at least as interesting as most biographies. The Gospels are not biographies; they are proclamations of Emmanuel, God with us. In the life of Jesus, we can see who God is and what it means to say that God is loving, merciful, just, compassionate, and open. There is more. In Jesus of Nazareth, we see who God is *and* who we can be. Jesus' absolute fidelity to God and his absolute commitment to all people reveal genuine possibilities for human life, for our own lives. It is in Jesus' fully human life that we discover what it means to "love the Lord your God with all your heart, and with all your soul, and with all your mind," and what it means to "love your neighbor as yourself" (Matthew 22:37, 39). Jesus Christ—in solidarity with both God and humankind—shows us who God is, and who God means us to be.

God is not an aloof deity, a mystery far beyond our comprehension. Jesus Christ is the reality of God's nearness: "It is the God who said, 'Let light shine out of darkness,' who has shone in our hearts to give the light of the knowledge of the glory of God in the face of Jesus Christ" (2 Corinthians 4:6). Jesus Christ is the Truth of God.

He Was Crucified, Dead, and Buried

It is in the death of Jesus that we come to understand the life of Jesus. Even a casual reading of the four Gospels shows that the evangelists consider Jesus' death to be of paramount importance. They recount in excruciating detail how he was betrayed and abandoned by his own disciples, then condemned by religious and political authorities. He was executed, dying the death of a common criminal alongside other common criminals. Somehow, we are told, he was crucified for us, dying for our sins. Since it is not immediately obvious what the death of Jesus has to do with us, Christians throughout the centuries have interpreted the crucifixion in various ways—Jesus was a sacrifice, Jesus suffered the punishment we deserve, Jesus was an example of self-giving love, Jesus defeated the power of sin and death, and so on.

These explanations of the meaning of Jesus' death do not always make sense to us. The language of sacrifice is alien, the notion of Jesus suffering punishment instead of us seems barbaric, the example of Jesus does not always inspire us, and the defeat of mysterious powers strikes us as mythical. Perhaps our attempt to understand the meaning of Christ's death should begin with the Gospel narratives themselves. As we read Matthew, Mark, Luke, and John, we see that Jesus' death is in complete continuity with his life. Jesus lived in the company of sinners, and that is how he died; flanked by criminals, he was executed as a criminal. In company with all who feel abandoned by God and by other people,

Jesus suffered in abandonment. In short, the absolute solidarity with people that characterized Jesus' life also characterized his death. God was in this Jesus who suffered physically, mentally, and emotionally. Moreover, in his death he suffered the end that comes to all people. Death is the end of human life, and this Jesus—God with us—identified himself fully with human life, including the absolute limit of human life.

If Jesus had only died with us, his solidarity with human life would be little more than divine confirmation of the empty end. Did God become one with us only to share our sometimes painful, sometimes tragic, sometimes ambiguous, but always final finish? If so, that might be good enough. To know that when we die we do not die alone, that God is with us in our loneliness, our suffering, and our fear would make a difference, wouldn't it? Is that all there is?

Like a somber drumbeat, the Apostles' Creed confesses that Jesus suffered, was crucified, died, was buried, and descended into hell. Dead, dead, really dead. Yet death was not the end. Jesus was raised from death to new life! "They put him to death by hanging him on a tree," the earliest Christian community proclaimed, "but God raised him on the third day and allowed him to appear . . . to us who were chosen by God as witnesses, and who ate and drank with him after he rose from the dead" (Acts 10:39-41). The risen Christ ate and drank with sinners. People began to realize that just as God had become one with us in the birth, life, and death of Jesus, so God makes us one with the risen Christ in new life. The early church affirmed that "just as Christ was raised from the dead by the glory of the Father, so we too might walk in newness of life. For if we have been united with him in a death like his, we will certainly be united with him in a resurrection like his" (Romans 6:4-5). God's identification with humankind did not end with the solidarity of death, but is renewed in new life—in this life and beyond death.

The first great creed of the church, the Nicene Creed (A.D. 325/381) sums up the gospel by confessing Jesus Christ as the only Son of the Father, whose incarnation, life, death, resurrection, ascension, and promised return are all *for us, for our sake:*

> We believe in one Lord, Jesus Christ,
> > the only Son of God,
> > eternally begotten of the Father,
> > God from God, Light from Light,
> > true God from true God,
> > begotten, not made,
> > of one Being with the Father;
> > through him all things were made.

For us and for our salvation
> he came down from heaven,
> was incarnate of the Holy Spirit and the Virgin Mary
> and became truly human.
> **For our sake** he was crucified under Pontius Pilate;
> he suffered death and was buried.
> On the third day he rose again
> in accordance with the Scriptures;
> he ascended into heaven
> and is seated at the right hand of the Father.
> He will come again in glory to judge the living and the dead,
> and his kingdom will have no end.

All for us, all for our sake: Knowing and believing this may bring fresh meaning to classical explanations of the meaning of Jesus' death.

- Sacrifice—not an attempt to satisfy a jealous god, but as the thankful, praise-filled offering of life to the creator of all life: *for us, for our sake.*

- Enduring punishment—not as the appeasement of an angry god, but as a supreme act of solidarity with us in our sin and guilt: *for us, for our sake.*

- The example of love—not as an object lesson for us to emulate, but as the ultimate expression of God's Way: *for us, for our sake.*

- The defeat of evil powers—not as the plot of a religious novel, but as liberation from all that seeks to diminish and control us: *for us, for our sake.*

The Confession of 1967 acknowledges that "God's reconciling act in Jesus Christ is a mystery which the Scriptures describe in various ways. . . . These are expressions of a truth which remains beyond the reach of all theory in the depths of God's love for humankind."[9] The full truth of incarnation, crucifixion, and resurrection remains beyond the reach of theory, but the truth is not inaccessible. Because it is all for us, for our sake, we can know, in the depth of our life, the truth of God's reconciling love in Jesus Christ.

Blessed Trinity?

As we listen to the Scriptures bear witness to the love of God made known to us in Jesus Christ through the power of the Holy Spirit, we hear about the Trinity: "One God, Father, Son, and Holy Spirit." Yet this central Christian affirmation has become an enigma to many church people who throw their hands up in despair when trying to explain the Trinity. How can one be three and three be one? Does it matter, anyway? Most of our problems with the doctrine of the Trinity come from attempting to understand God's inner being, trying to explain the nature of God. It is at that point that we find ourselves lost in inadequate analogies. Trinity is like H_2O, we are told, one substance that can take three forms—water, ice, and steam. Or, Trinity is like three interlocking circles that overlap to form a common center while retaining distinct areas. The analogies and symbols are not really helpful; at best, they are feeble attempts to express the inexpressible—the inner being of God. Moreover, even the best of the analogies do not help us to *know* God, to *love* God, to *live* as God's people. For too many Christians, Trinity has become an unnecessary puzzle that does not seem worth trying to solve.

Perhaps the problem is that we think of Trinity as a "doctrine," an intellectual formula, rather than an account of who God really is. It is often said that the Bible does not contain the doctrine of the Trinity. That is true enough, as far as it goes. Neither does Scripture contain the *doctrines* of creation, atonement, justification, sanctification, eschatology, or anything else. The Bible does not set forth doctrines, but rather narrates the presence of God through history, poetry, letters, prophecy, and other writings. Doctrines are our attempts to provide ordered accounts of the various biblical narratives of God with us. Scripture does not contain the *doctrine* of the Trinity, but it does contain a range of accounts that reveal the truth about God. This truth is best expressed as Trinity—as the one God who is Father, Son, and Holy Spirit.

Scripture tells the story of God with people through the stories of Israel, Jesus, and early Christian communities. Through these stories we come to know God as the loving Creator of all that is; as the gracious Reconciler of a divided, hostile world; and as the Builder and Sustainer of free human community. God's creating, reconciling, and community-sustaining actions are distinct, but they are not separate. The biblical story is not about a God who first created, then reconciled, then forged and sustained a faithful community. Nor is the story about a God who alternates among three disconnected works, now creating, now reconciling, now sustaining. The One God is eternally creating, reconciling, preserving. Thus, as God moves among us we know this One God in three distinct yet ever-actual and interconnected ways.

When we consider creation, we may focus on the loving work of "God the Father Almighty," yet the biblical witness is clear that creation is not the work of the Father apart from the Son and the Spirit. When we reflect on salvation, we may center on the loving work of Christ, yet the biblical witness is clear that salvation is not the work of the Son apart from the Father and the Spirit. When we think about the church, we may ponder the loving work of the Holy Spirit, yet the biblical witness is clear that the life of the redeemed community is not the work of the Spirit apart from the Son and the Father. All are the work of the one triune God, the action of God the Father through the Son in the power of the Holy Spirit.

Is our experience of God true to who God is? Or is our experience of God misleading, even deceiving? God makes God's very self known to us. Therefore, we can be confident that God *is* who we experience God to be in relation to us. The threefold manner in which God relates to us is a true manifestation of who God is as God! God's own being does not contradict the biblical story of God or the church's continuing experience of God. As God is to us, so God truly is—self-giving, loving, a community of sharing. The "names" we use for God's triunity—Father, Son, and Holy Spirit—connote inner relationships within the One God. God is Father in relation to the Son, Son in relation to the Father, Spirit in the loving bond of the unity of Father and Son. The Trinity is not philosophical speculation in search of reality. Trinity is the assurance that the God we know from the Scriptures and from the enduring experience of the community of faith is who God really is.

Throughout the narrative of God's Way in the world, Scripture is unself-conscious about the divinity of the Son and the Spirit and the essential unity of Father, Son, and Holy Spirit. Apparently, the biblical witnesses felt no need to argue a case, no need to explain how the reality of the one God is thoroughly consistent with differentiated action, and no need to develop a formally articulated doctrine of the Trinity. Instead, the Scriptures simply state the taken-for-granted presence of the one God in the grace of the Lord Jesus Christ, the love of God, and the communion of the Holy Spirit.

> Even though there may be so-called gods in heaven or on earth—as in fact there are many gods and many lords—yet for us there is one God, the Father, from whom are all things and for whom we exist, and one Lord, Jesus Christ, through whom are all things and through whom we exist.
>
> —1 Corinthians 8:5-6

> In the beginning was the Word, and the Word was with God, and the Word was God. He was in the beginning with God. All things came into being through him, and without him not one thing came into being.
>
> —John 1:1-3

> So [Christ] came and proclaimed peace to you who were far off and peace to those who were near; for through him both of us have access in one Spirit to the Father.
>
> —Ephesians 2:17-18

And when Jesus had been baptized, just as he came up from the water, suddenly the heavens were opened to him and he saw the Spirit of God descending like a dove and alighting on him. And a voice from heaven said, "This is my Son, the Beloved, with whom I am well pleased."

—Matthew 3:16-17

"I have said these things to you while I am still with you. But the Advocate, the Holy Spirit, whom the Father will send in my name, will teach you everything, and remind you of all that I have said to you."

—John 14:25-26

There is one body and one Spirit, just as you were called to the one hope of your calling, one Lord, one faith, one baptism, one God and Father of all, who is above all and through all and in all.

—Ephesians 4:4-6

These few scriptural sentences are not meant as proofs, or even as a catalog of Trinitarian references. They simply illustrate the natural way Scripture assumes the integrity of the triune God whose actions in the world are a differentiated whole.

While the New Testament does not set out a developed Trinitarian Christology, the Scriptures are clear that Jesus is more than a teacher and prophet: "In Christ God was reconciling the world to himself" (2 Corinthians 5:19); "For in him all the fullness of God was pleased to dwell, and through him God was pleased to reconcile to himself all things, whether on earth or in heaven, by making peace through the blood of his cross" (Colossians 1:19-20).

The New Testament does not elaborate a Trinitarian doctrine of the Holy Spirit, but the Scriptures are clear that the Holy Spirit is more than human spirituality writ large: "the spirit of glory, which is the Spirit of God, is resting on you" (1 Peter 4:14); "Now the Lord is the Spirit, and where the Spirit of the Lord is, there is freedom" (2 Corinthians 3:17).

The New Testament does not elaborate a Trinitarian theology, but Scripture is clear that God is the Father of the Son, the Son of the Father, and the Spirit of God and the Spirit of Christ, in relationships of love that flow into the world: "When the Advocate comes, whom I will send to you from the Father, the Spirit of truth who comes from the Father, he will testify on my behalf" (John 15:26).

It may come as a surprise to realize that there is only one New Testament instance of Father, Son, and Holy Spirit occurring together—"Go therefore and make disciples of all nations, baptizing them in the name of the Father and of the Son and of the Holy Spirit, and teaching them to obey everything that I have commanded you" (Matthew 28:19-20). This does not minimize the centrality of

Trinitarian expression in the New Testament; it only confirms the natural, unself-conscious, non-dogmatic way in which Scripture articulates faith in the triune God.

God is present to us—in divine self-giving and in our common experience—as one God who is Father, Son, and Holy Spirit. "Unless we grasp these," says Calvin, "only the bare and empty name of God flits about in our brains, to the exclusion of the true God."[10] "God" can mean almost anything to anyone (in Ingolf Dalferth's memorable phrase, "I determine what God is"). To know God's presence among us as Father, Son, and Holy Spirit is to know *this* God, not any god. We cannot presume that our doctrine of the triune God is an exhaustive definition of "God as God is," for God remains free from the confines of human language, but we can be confident that God relates to us as God is. Once again, Calvin's notion of God's accommodation is helpful: God shares God's true being in a way that we can comprehend.

Knowing that God's threefold relatedness to the world is the truth about the being of God does more than get our doctrine straight. In confessing the triune being of God we find assurance that the life of God is not remote and isolated, inaccessible to us. God not only acts in self-giving, affirming, community-building ways—God *is* self-giving, mutually affirming, community-building love. Thus, our experience of God's love is not merely an experience of something God does, but an experience of *God*. As God does, so God is. Moreover, since God is who God is *in relation to us*, we are invited to share the very life of God as we live lives of self-giving, mutually affirming, community-building love.

Trinitarian understandings of God and God's Way in the world are radically different from general ideas about "divinity." Our understanding of *sovereignty* is changed from remote governance to loving care for all creation. God's *power* is transformed from the coercion of dominant force into the dynamic reign of relationships in love. God's *salvation* is no longer a legal transaction, but a gracious restoration of communion. God's *new community* is neither a collective nor an assemblage of individuals, but the presence of open mutuality. As God does, so God is . . . and so we are invited to do and be as we share in the very life of God.

If we say the Trinity remains a "mystery," it is not because God and God's Way are unfathomable, but only because our thoughts and words are never adequate to express fully who we know God to be and what God does among us. Nevertheless, we can dispense with both despair and arcane speculation, knowing that the community's ongoing experience of God's Way in the world is a genuine experience of the One God, Father, Son, and Holy Spirit. The "mystery" of the Trinity is that the more we know about the one God, Father, Son, and Holy Spirit, the more we know that there is more to be known.

The Language Problem

Our problems with Trinity are not confined to inadequate analogies, doctrinal abstractions, or deep mystery. Many contemporary Christians have difficulty with the language of Trinity, specifically the gender specificity of Father-Son, and the use of the male pronouns *he*, *him*, and *himself* in reference to God. The church does not use Father-Son language merely because it is scriptural and creedal language, although this is not an insignificant consideration. Scripture bears witness to Jesus, who is identified by the voice of God: "You are my Son, the Beloved." Scripture bears witness to God, who is identified by Jesus as "my Father." Moreover, the relationship is characterized in terms of mutual knowledge: "No one knows who the Son is except the Father, or who the Father is except the Son and anyone to whom the Son chooses to reveal him" (Luke 10:22). (Even the Jesus Seminar, voting with colored marbles, identifies as "certain" Jesus' reference to God as Father. The only word of the Lord's Prayer that the Jesus Seminar is convinced came from Jesus' lips is "Father."[11]) Throughout the centuries the creeds of the church have made consistent confession of one God, Father, Son, and Holy Spirit. Setting aside Scripture and creed—and, more important, setting aside the words of Jesus whom we confess to be God with us—is not something to be done lightly, however admirable the motivation.

The more important reason for the church's retention of Father-Son-Spirit language—and perhaps the reason that occasioned it in the first place—is that the language is both relational and personal. Unlike, for example, "Creator, Redeemer, and Sustainer," Father-Son-Spirit language is relational. Fathers have sons; sons have fathers; fathers and sons have and are bound in common spirit. On the other hand, creators do not have redeemers, redeemers do not have creators, and creators and redeemers do not have sustainers. Language for Trinity must be relational, not merely functional. Similarly, language for Trinity must be personal. Rock, cornerstone, and temple are biblical images that, while suggesting a certain relationship, are impersonal.

Trinitarian language is not confined to Father-Son-Spirit language. A theological statement on the doctrine of the Trinity, received by the Presbyterian Church (U.S.A.), affirms Father, Son, and Holy Spirit as foundational, an indispensable anchor, the root from which all language about God grows. The theological statement also acknowledges other faithful articulations that come from the deep tradition of the church: Speaker-Word-Breath, Sun-Ray-Warmth, Giver-Gift-Giving. None of these is adequate in itself; none is a replacement of Father, Son, and Holy Spirit; and none is intended as a form of address to God. Yet all are helpful supplements to the fully personal, relational language of Scripture and tradition.

One final observation is in order. Father-Son-Spirit is explicitly Trinitarian language, language that expresses Trinitarian relationships. It is not intended as pervasive and exclusive language for God. It is as inappropriate to address God exclusively as "Father" as it is to refer to Trinity as "Creator-Redeemer-Sustainer." "Father" is the name used in relation to the Son, and in relation to our adoption through the Son, not a generic title for God. When we speak of the one triune God, rather than of the Trinitarian relations, we are free to use language that expresses the full range of biblical images. Long before "inclusive language" became an issue in the church, John Calvin noted that "God did not satisfy himself with proposing the example of a father, but in order to express his strong affection, he chose to liken himself to a mother, and calls [the people of Israel] not merely 'children,' but *the fruit of the womb*, towards which there is usually a warmer affection."[12]

Scripture displays a wealth of language for God. Some of the scriptural language is central while other language is peripheral. The biblical witness to God employs rich metaphors, straightforward similes, and simple images as well as the central language of name and narrative. Christian use of language for God should be as full as the Scriptures and should distinguish between language that is central and pervasive and language that is occasional and peripheral.

One Lord, One Faith, One Baptism, One God and Father of All

It often seems that differing understandings of the gospel hopelessly fragment Christians. These days, denominational distinctions are complicated by theological and ideological divisions within denominations, further fracturing the Christian community. Yet we can still speak of a *Christian community*, for we are united in the common convictions that God has given himself to humankind in Jesus Christ, and that we can trust God's self-revelation as Father, Son, and Holy Spirit. While it is true that all Christians do not always agree on interpretations of these two central affirmations, their different insights occur within shared convictions; these truths bind us together in one faith. Perhaps deep dialogues about shared faith would better serve the ecumenical task of the churches than attention to differences in matters of faith and order.

1. P. D. James, *The Children of Men* (New York: Vintage, 1992), p. 173.
2. Eileen Lindner, ed., *Yearbook of American and Canadian Churches* (New York: National Council of the Churches of Christ in the U.S.A., 2008).
3. Jean-Jacques Bauswein and Lukas Vischer, eds., *The Reformed Family Worldwide* (Grand Rapids: Eerdmans Publishing, 1999).
4. N. T. Wright, "The Biblical Formation of a Doctrine of God," in *Who Do You Say That I Am? Christology and the Church*, ed. Donald Armstrong (Grand Rapids: Eerdmans, 1999), p. 50.
5. For a fuller treatment of the Christian response to religious pluralism, see Joseph D. Small, *Preservation of the Truth* (Louisville: Witherspoon Press, 2005), pp. 53–68.
6. Calvin, *Institutes*, 1.17.13., p. 227.
7. *Institutes*, 1.13.1., p. 121.
8. John H. Leith, ed., "The Definition of Chalcedon," in *Creeds of the Church* (Garden City: Anchor, 1963), p. 35.
9. *The Confession of 1967: Inclusive Language Text* (Louisville: Office of Theology and Worship, 2002), 9.09.
10. *Institutes*, 1.13.2., p. 122
11. Robert Funk, *The Five Gospels: What Did Jesus Really Say?* (New York: HarperCollins, 1997), p. 148.
12. Calvin, *Commentary on Isaiah 49:15*.

5

Protestant Principles

At the age of twenty I thought that Luther had given us a gift of hope. It didn't take me long to understand that he had immediately sold it back to the powerful. The old friar freed us from the Pope and the bishops, but he condemned us to expiate sin in solitude, in the solitude of internal anguish, putting a priest in our souls, a court in our consciences . . . Luther stripped the priests of their black garb, only to put it on the hearts of all men.

Luther Blissett, Q[1]

The worldwide Christian community is united in common profession of one God, Father, Son, and Holy Spirit, known to us clearly in the incarnation, life, death, and resurrection of Jesus Christ. Unfortunately, the worldwide Christian community is also fragmented, divided into countless traditions, churches, denominations, and sects. Perhaps we can begin to make sense of the profusion of churches by noting that the one holy catholic apostolic church is divided into four great branches: Roman Catholic, Orthodox, Protestant, and Pentecostal. (Some observers contend that Anglicans, known in the United States as Episcopalians, are another major branch that bridges the gap between Roman Catholics and Protestants.) Each of these ecclesial expressions bears a distinct tradition with characteristic forms of theology, liturgy, and ministry.

The long history of Christian division can be recounted briefly enough. As Christian faith spread throughout the Roman Empire, differences developed between the Latin-speaking West, centered in Rome, and the Greek-speaking East, centered in Constantinople. Distinct theological emphases, differences in worship and forms of piety, and disparate understandings of church order led to formal schism in 1054, complete with declarations of anathema and mutual excommunication. Only in the twentieth century was significant contact established between the Eastern Orthodox churches and the churches of the West.

The Western, Roman Catholic branch of the church fell on hard times in medieval Europe. Abuse of church power, corruption of the papacy, aberrations in popular piety, and theological extravagance led to repeated attempts at reform. Long before Martin Luther burst on the scene in 1519, Pope Gregory VII, Bernard of Clairvaux, Francis of Assisi, John Wyclif, Jan Hus, and many others worked to cleanse the church of mistaken practices, returning it to more faithful thought and life. Reform of the Catholic Church, not separation from it, was also the desire of Luther, Calvin, and other early reformers. Their intention was positive—a restoration of the good news of Jesus Christ—and they were disappointed that their efforts led to division within the church. They were also disappointed that differences within the reform movement led to the proliferation of distinct, separate churches.

We are accustomed to think of Luther, Calvin, and other sixteenth-century reformers as firebrands who rejected the Catholic Church with enflamed rhetoric and bitter invective. Their censure of the Catholic Church and its practices was virtually without exception, yet the purpose of their critique was always reform, not schism. In a remarkable letter to Thomas Cranmer, archbishop of Canterbury, Calvin agonized,

> This other thing also is to be ranked among the chief evils of our time, viz., that the Churches are so divided, that human fellowship is scarcely now in any repute among us . . . Thus it is that the members of the Church being severed, the body lies bleeding. So much does this concern me, that, could I be of any service, I would not grudge to cross even ten seas, if need were, on account of it.[2]

He also wrote to the Reformed churches in France about his conviction that a universal council of the Church was necessary to put an end to the divisions in Christendom. Calvin was willing to include the Catholic bishops in the council, as long as it also included elected persons who desired and demanded the reform of the Church. He was even open to the possibility that the pope would preside (but not rule) over the deliberations of the council.[3]

The hopes of the reformers were not realized. Within a generation the Protestant movement had splintered into four major branches—Lutheran, Reformed, Anabaptist, and Anglican—which became increasingly distant from, and often hostile to, one another. In turn, these branches have splintered repeatedly. Church divisions are sometimes healed, but most have endured, so that denominationalism is simply "the way things are" for most contemporary Christians. Moreover, there persists a strong impulse to divide further the already divided churches whenever disagreements emerge over doctrines or morals. Many Protestant denominations in the United States currently face the threat or the reality of splitting apart, most notably the Presbyterian Church (U.S.A.), the Episcopal Church, and the Southern Baptist Convention.

We live in an odd ecclesial culture. The North American reality of multiple denominations seems normal to us, but that is because the existence of numerous denominations is all we have ever known. Congregations of different denominations as well as nondenominational congregations usually coexist, sometimes cooperate, but often compete with one another for members! What the world sees in North America is an array of churches that look and act like marketplace commodities. Denominations regularly advertise themselves in national media campaigns, differentiating themselves from other churches by targeting niche markets. Congregations engage in local promotions, peddling a full range of religious goods and services. At all levels, churches put themselves forward as the best option for meeting the real and imagined needs of the shrinking number of religion's consumers. These efforts are often called "evangelism," but they have less to do with the good news of salvation in Christ than with the marketing of full-service religious institutions. The churches turn mission away from the world and inward upon themselves, existing mainly to serve the collective needs of their new and old members while competing with one another for market share in a declining demographic. Far from proclaiming the gospel, the churches proclaim themselves, without a hint of discomfort or embarrassment.

None of this would have seemed normal to the reformers. The proliferation of separated traditions, churches, denominations, and congregations would have appalled Calvin, Luther, and other leaders of the Reformation. While it was possible for them to conceive of distinct churches living in different geographical locations, a multitude of Christian churches existing side by side within a locality was beyond their worst imagining.

However we appraise it, the fragmentation of the church is the reality we have. Nevertheless, in spite of historic and continuing divisions, certain commonalities make it possible to speak of the Protestant tradition. Protestantism is not a sharply defined, cohesive institution, but it is an identifiable reality on the ecclesial landscape. Three shared affirmations stand out as markers of Protestant conviction: the primacy of the Bible in matters of faith and practice, justification by grace through faith, and the priesthood of all believers. These affirmations, which continue to shape the faith and life of Protestant churches, are not foreign to Roman Catholicism and Eastern Orthodoxy, particularly in our time. They remain distinctive emphases of Protestantism, allowing us to claim a common heritage.

The Bible

Not too long ago, most Bibles were printed on gold-edged, tissue-thin paper, bound in black leather. Today, Bibles come in all shapes and sizes in a bewildering array of translations and paraphrases. Specialized "study Bible" editions are produced to cater to every demographic category. Yet, in spite of the unprecedented availability of the Scriptures, the Bible remains a mystery to many people, a neglected artifact of Christian faith. For decades, Christian leaders have been lamenting "the strange silence of the Bible in the church." On the face of it, disregard of Scripture seems odd. The Confession of 1967 eloquently describes the indispensability of the Bible:

> The one sufficient revelation of God is Jesus Christ, the Word of God incarnate, to whom the Holy Spirit bears unique and authoritative witness through the Holy Scriptures, which are received and obeyed as the word of God written. The Scriptures are not a witness among others, but the witness without parallel. The church has received the books of the Old and New Testaments as prophetic and apostolic testimony in which it hears the Word of God and by which its faith and obedience are nourished and regulated.[4]

The confession makes sweeping claims for Scripture, not only as a rule of faith and life, but also as the Word of God by which the Holy Spirit gives access to the truth of Christ. Why is it, then, that writings central to Christian faith are so peripheral to the lives of so many church members?

At the most basic level, problems of *understandability* confront today's readers. How can we make sense out of a book that is really a collection of at least sixty-six different documents written over a span of centuries? We read Old Testament prophets and become lost in a sea of obscure historical references. We read Paul's letters in the New Testament and find ourselves struggling to understand puzzling words and intricate arguments. The book of Revelation takes us on a magical mystery tour of indecipherable symbols. So much of the Bible is hard to figure out. How many Christians have vowed to read the Bible from beginning to end, only to abandon the effort midway through Leviticus? The Scriptures seem too hard to understand, so Bibles are ignored or dusted off for an occasional Lenten study.

Our neglect of the Bible has deeper roots than problems of understanding. It takes hard work to understand how to use sophisticated computer software programs and how to navigate the Internet, but people make the effort because it seems worthwhile. We do not give comparable effort to the Bible because we have questions about the Bible's *relevance*. The issues we face are not the same as the issues addressed in the Old and New Testaments. What does King David's conquest of the Philistines have to do with contemporary international affairs? Does Jesus' healing of sick people tell us anything about modern health care? Where does the Bible address contemporary social issues such as reform of the welfare system and educational policy, or personal concerns such as depression, divorce, and career choices? Even if we understand the Bible, we are struck by seemingly huge gaps between its contents and our lives.

Our doubts about the Bible's relevance are sharpened by questions about *how the Bible is used*. "You can prove anything from the Bible," people say cynically. What they really mean is that *nothing* can be proved by quoting verses from the Scriptures.

Every citation on one side of an issue can be matched by a citation on the other side. Is abortion's rightness or wrongness proved by quoting an isolated verse from Jeremiah? Can disagreements about homosexuality be decided by interpreting a handful of verses scattered throughout the Old and New Testaments? Using the Bible as if it were *Bartlett's Familiar Quotations* is a game that people play, but many of us do not wish to join.

Doubts about the Bible's understandability, relevance, and use climax in the fundamental question of *authority*. Even if we understand fully the Old Testament book of Obadiah, determine that it is relevant to our time, and identify a passage that expresses a clear position on an important issue, we are uncertain about the weight it bears in the decisions we must make. Does the Bible override all other considerations and overrule all other authorities? When we have determined "what the Bible says," is the matter closed? Are there other authorities that stand alongside us as we think matters through? What weight should be given to our experience, the findings of science, history, different cultures, and more?

The ways in which the "historical-critical" method of interpreting Scripture has filtered down to the church complicate our difficulties with the Bible. Historical-critical examination of the Bible focuses on linguistic, historical, source, and genre examination of biblical texts. An unfortunate result of the historical-critical method has been to convince ordinary Christians that only scholars are equipped to interpret texts. The knowledge needed to engage the Bible with the scholarly tools of interpretation is beyond the capacity of most church members and many ministers. An even more devastating result of historical-critical interpretation has been to convince many ordinary Christians that the Bible is only a record of what people used to believe centuries ago. Viewing the prophets or Paul simply in terms of their own times and places can relegate Scripture to the status of a classic, like Homer's *Odyssey* and *Iliad* or Dante's *Inferno*. If only scholars have the erudition to discern the beliefs of ages past, why should people make the effort to engage in amateur examination of ancient views and values?

Given the difficulties we encounter with the Bible, it is small wonder that so many Christians spend so little time reading it. Yet Protestant churches have always been united in affirming that this book lies at the center of Christian faith. The reformers were not less sophisticated than we are; they were familiar with problems of the Bible's understandability, relevance, use, and authority. They, too, were responsible interpreters who took account of historical and literary contexts. Yet for them, and for countless ordinary Christians since their time, the Bible has been an incomparable guide to faith and life, God's Word to us.

Once again, Calvin provides us with a delightful image that may help us to understand the Bible's place in faith and life. As we look around us at the world, our own experience, other people, and the problems that confront us, we try to make sense of it all. We try to understand who God is, who we are, and how we are to live. Do we see everything clearly? Clearly, we do not. Calvin notes what many of us know from personal experience: "Eyes, when dimmed with age or weakness or by some other defect, unless aided by spectacles, discern nothing distinctly." He then draws an analogy between imperfect physical vision and our insight into the truth about God and ourselves: "So, such is our feebleness, unless Scripture guides us in seeking God, we are immediately confused."[5] The Bible is our God-given pair of eyeglasses, the lenses that bring into clear focus who God is, who we are, and how we can live, making it possible to see God's world clearly. The Bible is not an ancient substitute for our experience or an encyclopedia that eliminates all other authorities, but the "spectacles" through which we can see clearly the Way of God in the world.

As our corrective lenses, the Scriptures are what we look *through* more than something we look *at*. The books of the Bible tell the story of God with people. From ancient Israel to the early church, from David to Paul, from Miriam to Phoebe, from Exodus to Pentecost, the Bible recounts God's self-disclosure in the lives of people. As their experiences are related, we are presented with the possibility that these narratives are more than stories from the past—they disclose to us God's continuing presence in the life of the world. The Scriptures are not history lessons, coded messages, rule books, or philosophical essays; they are the accounts of God with people that provide the lenses though which we are able to see the present reality of God with us more clearly.

Why this book and not others? What makes these writings unique and authoritative for us? Throughout the centuries, people have discovered that these writings really do enable us to see clearly. Thus, the church has confirmed that the Scriptures are the corrective lenses that bring the reality of God into focus, making it possible to perceive the truth about the life of the world. The church's affirmation that the Bible enables clear insight into the truth has also led it to recognize that the Bible is an instance of God's gracious accommodation to us. God has ensured that people have available to them a truthful account of God's Way in the world. God has provided the glasses we need to see things as they are.

We need not claim that the Scriptures are scientifically precise nor must we devise theories of biblical inerrancy to recognize that these writings are the "unique and authoritative witness . . . the witness without parallel,"[6] and that they encompass the "whole counsel of God, concerning all things necessary for his own glory, man's salvation, faith, and life."[7] In a clever variation on Calvin's image of spectacles, Frederick Buechner says,

If you look *at* a window, you see flyspecks, dust, the crack where Junior's Frisbee hit it. If you look *through* a window, you see the world beyond.

Something like this is the difference between those who see the Bible as a Holy Bore and those who see it as the Word of God which speaks out of the depths of an almost unimaginable past into the depths of ourselves.[8]

It may be that too much Bible study in the church is confined to looking at the *window*, examining the *eyeglasses*. The purpose of Bible study goes beyond mastering facts of ancient history and comprehending unfamiliar forms of thought. We read and study to gain a clearer vision of God, of ourselves, and of God's new Way in the world. If our study is limited to understanding the instrument, we may miss the broad vision that the instrument can help us to see. In too many churches and theological schools, study of Scripture is turned into intellectual archaeology, digging through the past to discover what people used to believe. While study of the Scriptures must preserve the integrity of the writings' particular times and places, we read and study in the conviction that biblical narratives, prayers, letters, and other writings are not imprisoned in the distant past. The Hebrews whom God rescued from slavery and the squabbling Corinthians to whom Paul wrote are not mere displays in the museum of God's former days. Neither are we those Hebrews and Corinthians, mere recapitulations of the story of God and people. Instead, the accounts of God's movement among the people of Israel and the early Christian community provide us with a window on the world—God's world—letting us see beyond the little room of our own time and place. With vision restored, we can see God's Way in our own time and place accurately and honestly.

Sola scriptura is a misunderstood watchword of the Reformation. It does not mean "only Scripture, to the exclusion of everything else." Instead, *sola scriptura* means that Scripture is the supreme norm by which we measure Christian faith and life. Belief that is in accord with Scripture properly articulates the truth about God and ourselves. Behaviors that are in accord with Scripture properly enact God's new Way in the world. *Sola scriptura* has never meant that Christians should ignore everything else, including the tradition of the church, only that all else, including tradition, is accountable to Scripture's authoritative witness to the truth about God and God's Way. This means, of course, that Scripture is potentially set in judgment over the tradition as well as over our personal views and preferences. The church can err and individual Christians can err; it is Scripture that judges and corrects human error.

Historically, Protestant churches have been united in their conviction that Scripture is uniquely authoritative in ecclesial life and personal discipleship. In our own time, however, many Protestant churches experience bitter internal debates over the nature of the Bible's inspiration and the character of its authority. It may be telling that debates about the Bible occur at a time when reading of the Bible has waned. Reformation of the church has always grown from recovery of the

Scriptures by the church. The task of Protestant churches today is not to perfect an agreed-upon doctrine of Scripture, but to renew the reading of Scripture.

Justification by Grace through Faith

When we look at life through the lens of the Bible, we recognize that aspects of our experience are brought into focus. How, for instance, do we perceive the relationship between God and us? The Bible makes clear what we already sense is true: God is God and we are humans. "For my thoughts are not your thoughts, nor are your ways my ways, says the LORD. For as the heavens are higher than the earth, so are my ways higher than your ways and my thoughts than your thoughts" (Isaiah 55:8–9). How can the gap be bridged between the One who is "wholly other" and mere mortals?

Martin Luther was a German monk who felt intensely the distance between the Holy God and his own flawed self. Luther's agonized question was how a sinful human could satisfy the righteous demands of a holy God. Luther knew that the law of God makes clear what God requires of us: to love God with all our heart, soul, mind, and strength, and to love our neighbors as ourselves. Yet Luther also knew that we do not fulfill the law, that we cannot fulfill it. No matter how hard we try, the law always shows us how far short we fall. We stand condemned by the law, unable by effort of will to meet its demands, unable to approach a holy God, unable to live in a way that merits the love of God. No one is good enough. Moreover, Luther understood that even our continual repentance and acts of penance cannot compensate for our transgressions of God's law. We find ourselves caught in a futile cycle of sin and penance that can never overcome our self-imposed distance from God.

As Luther read the Scriptures, he discovered that the Bible displayed a startlingly different view of the relationship between God and people. We do not have to strive to acquit ourselves of our guilt before a righteous God! We do not have to work to atone for our failings to satisfy God's righteousness! Why not? Because God's gracious love has bridged the gap between God and us in Jesus Christ, justifying us when we could not justify ourselves. We are saved from sin, guilt, and separation by the grace of God. As we trust in the good news that God's mercy has done what we cannot do, we are drawn close to God, enabled to live in trusting freedom. "Since these promises of God are holy, true, righteous, free and peaceful words, full of goodness," says Luther, "the soul which clings to them with a firm faith will be so closely united with them and altogether absorbed by them that it not only will share in all their power but will be saturated and intoxicated by them."[9]

For Luther, as for Calvin after him, the relationship between God and humankind was often expressed in legal images: law, guilt, penance, atonement, justification, righteousness. Legal images may not be as meaningful to us. The contemporary American legal system has as much to do with the assertion of rights as with the acknowledgment of duties, with relief as with punishment, with compensation as with penalties. We often view the law as a system that will guarantee us what we are due rather than a code that will hold us accountable for what we do! Even if we understand the law as a code of duties and prohibitions, legal requirements are rarely straightforward. Too often, the legal system is a labyrinth that may trap us unfairly or provide people with a route to secure advantage for themselves.

The Reformation's insights are not dependent upon the legal terms in which they are expressed. While it is not wrong to see the gap between God and humankind as the distance between righteousness and transgression, we are not restricted to this one way of recognizing that a gap has been bridged by God in Christ, that God's grace creates new life that we cannot produce, that our trust in the promises of God brings about a relationship that we cannot manufacture. The Bible displays an array of pictures that reveal God's grace. Beyond justification we can see God's love for us as release from bondage to sin and death, adoption as God's children, reconciliation, restored communion, new birth, friendship with God, and more.

The great insight of the Protestant Reformation is that God's love for humankind is expressed in God's gracious coming to us when we could not approach him. God's grace is too rich to be confined within one means of expression. Our experience of faith is too deep to be captured in a single phrase. The good news is that God's initiative creates a new human reality and that our trust in God is the way of living that new reality. We are saved by grace through faith. We are saved for a life of loving God with all that we are, and for loving others fully.

The Priesthood of All Believers

If the distance between God and us is bridged by God's gracious initiative, and if we receive God's grace in trust, there is no need to place procedures or people between God and us. "Now we, who have been baptized, are all uniformly priests in virtue of that very fact."[10] It was Luther's revolutionary notion that all Christians do their own believing, without need for a special class of Christians to mediate their faith in God. The heart of believers' priesthood lies in their capacity and responsibility for their faith and faithfulness: "Each and all of us are priests because we have the one faith, the one gospel, one and the same sacrament; why, then, should we not be entitled to taste or test, and to judge what is right or wrong in the faith?"[11]

Who among us doubts it? We Protestants are quite certain that popes cannot tell us what to believe. We are equally certain that our own church assemblies cannot tell us what to believe and that pastors of congregations cannot tell members what to believe. We are equally certain that our faith is not tied to requirements of regular worship, generous stewardship, and sacrificial service. Our beliefs are *our* beliefs, after all, and we can believe whatever we please. Each of us may have different beliefs, of course, but that is our right, isn't it? No one can coerce our conscience! Is this radical individualism of belief what the Reformers meant by the priesthood of believers?

Protestant churches have always recognized that Christians do their own believing, free from coercion by ecclesiastical dogma or priestly office. "God alone is Lord of the conscience," the Presbyterian *Book of Order* states, "and hath left it free from the doctrines and commandments of men." Yet this is not to say that *we* are the lords of our own consciences. It is not to imagine that belief is a matter of personal preference or that it doesn't matter what we believe. We are free from blind obedience to those doctrines and commandments "which are in anything contrary to [God's] Word, or beside it, in matters of faith or worship."[12] Are we free to ignore "doctrines and commandments" that are *faithful* to God's Word? The great Protestant affirmation of the priesthood of all believers brings us back to the foundational conviction that the Bible is the lens through which we can perceive the truth about God, about us, and about how we can live.

Individual license to believe anything is not freedom, but imprisonment within a solitary, windowless cell. The Bible is our window on the world through which we can see the truth about God, about ourselves, and about life. It is through the lens of Scripture that we are free to behold and trust the gospel of God's grace in Jesus Christ through the power of the Holy Spirit. We do not need other people to tell us what the gospel is; we can see it for ourselves. We do not need rigid rules to circumscribe faithful living; we can live the good news for ourselves. Yet it is the *gospel* that we are to see and live, not a philosophy of our own devising or an ethic that suits our desires. The freedom to do our own believing is the liberty to receive the truth about God, about ourselves, and about God's Way in the world.

We do our own believing, but we do not believe alone. In the *priesthood* of all believers we are not solitary priests, but priests with and to one another. St. Augustine, a great theologian and bishop of the early church, recounts a puzzling experience in his *Confessions*. During a visit to Milan, he saw the bishop, Ambrose, doing something odd: reading silently. Why, Augustine wondered, would Ambrose read to himself, with silent voice and tongue? Was he trying to preserve his weak voice? Or did he know that if he read aloud he would be asked too many questions?[13] In Augustine's time as in much of the church's life, the normal way of reading the Bible was aloud, in a group. Reading the Bible led to questions, discussion, exploration. Christians would gather at this window on the world, telling each other what they saw, pointing out to each other features of the landscape, helping one another appreciate the view. The vista of the gospel is too wide for any one of us to see it all. Together, acting as priests with one another, we can see more than we could if restricted to our own vision.

The Protestant tradition frees us from the compulsion of ecclesiastical authority, but it does not leave us in solitude. It places us within a community of believers that looks and listens, speaks and acts, together. The Bible is the community's book. As men and women who are justified by God's grace through faith, we are placed within a new community of freedom. This new community is one in which we serve one another. The foundational form of our mutual service is helping one another trust the good news of Jesus Christ. Only then can we proclaim this good news to people who have not yet heard it. Only then can we engage in joyful service to a world in desperate need.

The Protestant Principle

Protestantism is hardly a unified phenomenon. The differences among myriad denominations are obvious and real. Even the three common affirmations—the primacy of the Bible, justification by grace through faith, and the priesthood of all believers—are maintained differently within the spectrum of Protestant church life. Southern Baptists and Episcopalians do not view the Bible in the same way. Justification by grace is presented one way in a Billy Graham crusade, in another way in Lutheran worship. The priesthood of believers within a community of faith works out differently for Pentecostals and Methodists.

Perhaps intra-Protestant differences result from what Paul Tillich called the "Protestant Principle"—the refusal to exalt anything human to the level of ultimate concern, the protest against any absolute claim made for a relative reality.[14] Thus, no human formulation of Christian faith can ever be given unqualified assent. Yet this essentially negative understanding of the "Protestant Principle" obscures the original meaning of the word *protest*, derived from the Latin *protestari*. At the time of the Reformation, "to protest" did not mean to object or dissent, but rather "to profess," or "to declare openly." Historically, Protestants have professed their understanding of the gospel confidently even as they resist every effort to grant ultimate authority to human formulations of God's truth.

It may be that "Protestantism" in North America and Europe now experiences a certain lack of confidence in its profession of the gospel. The Bible is often an object of skeptical debate or the subject of intradenominational conflict rather than the source of good news. Justification by grace though faith strikes many as a concept that is out of place in a consumer-oriented society and an increasingly consumer-oriented church. Within institutionalized church structures, the priesthood of all believers is concealed beneath ecclesiastical regulations and bureaucratic procedures.

The recovery of Protestant confidence may lie with the recovery of distinctive Protestant affirmations. The Reformation cry, *ad fontes* (to the sources), expressed the need to strip away accumulated cultural and institutional overlays that had concealed the faith and faithfulness of the gospel. Revisiting Scripture with eyes ready to see and ears ready to hear, rediscovering the deep tradition of the church as a faithful guide to the biblical witness, and reappropriating patterns of life that gave shape to dedicated discipleship were elements of the Reformation's return to the sources that had as its goal the church's return to Christ, *the Source* of its life. Contemporary Protestant churches may return to their Reformation sources by renewed attention to Scripture, the gospel of our justification, and the shape of life in the community of faith.

The Ecumenical Imperative

Calvin, Luther, and other early reformers worked for the reform of the church, not its division. Even when they recognized the need for different churches in different geographical locations, and even when they engaged in sharp disputes among themselves, they always understood that the restored unity of the church was a gospel imperative. Luther and Calvin would be horrified by the fragmentation of the churches that resulted from their attempts to renew the one holy catholic apostolic church, and mortified to hear their efforts at reform being used to justify continuous schism.

In 1539, when the Reformation was still in its early stages, Cardinal Sadoleto, a French bishop, wrote a letter to the government and citizens of Geneva, imploring them to return to the Catholic Church. In his letter, Sadoleto contrasted fifteen centuries of Catholic unity with the current division of the church and the profusion of differing "sects" spawned by the reformers: "For already, since these men began, how many sects have torn the Church? Sects not agreeing with them, yet disagreeing with each other—a manifest indication of falsehood."[15] A young John Calvin replied to Sadoleto by acknowledging that the most serious of the charges against the reformers was "that we have attempted to dismember the Spouse of Christ. Were that true, both you and the whole world might regard us as desperate." Calvin acknowledged the reality of divisions within the church, but denied that responsibility lay with the proponents of reformation. "I admit that, on the revival of the gospel, great disputes arose where all was quietness before. But that is unjustly imputed to our [reformers], who, during the whole course of their proceedings, desired nothing more than that religion being revived, the Churches, which discord had scattered and dispersed, might be gathered together into true unity."[16]

The scattering has continued unabated, and true unity still falls prey to discord. Shortly before his death, Jesus prayed for his disciples—his disciples then *and now*— "I ask not only on behalf of these, but also on behalf of those who will believe in me through their word, that they may all be one. As you, Father, are in me and I am in you, may they also be in us, so that the world may believe that you have sent me . . . that they may become completely one, so that the world may know that you have sent me and have loved them even as you have loved me" (John 17:20–23). The unity of the real church is not merely a matter of ecclesiastical diplomacy, or even of inter-church communion. It is a feature of the integrity of the gospel, an imperative for the divided churches. The need for the visible oneness of the Christian community is not for the sake of the church. Christian unity is for the sake of the world, for the sake of those who do not know that God has sent the Beloved into the world and who do not know that the Father loves them as he loves the Son. Jesus' prayer expresses the link between the unity of the church, the world's knowledge that the Father has sent the Son, and the world's assurance that the Father's love for the world is grounded in the mutual love of the Father and the Son.

Not that long ago, churches asserted their superiority over other churches. Denominations stressed their distinctive doctrine and governance in opposition to the theological and organizational life of other denominations. Thankfully, unpleasant denominational triumphalism is a receding memory for most churches in North America. It has been replaced by an unprecedented openness to one another, characterized by cordial relationships at every level of church life. This new openness is partially composed of bourgeois American tolerance, postmodern uncertainty, and confessional minimalism, but it also represents a genuine willingness to recognize each other as authentic expressions of the one church of Jesus Christ. Generous openness to the other has not led to urgent engagements that might create genuine recognizable unity. The world still sees "Christianity" in a fractured, dizzying kaleidoscope image of differentiated church institutions: Orthodox, Catholic, Protestant, and Pentecostal—each separated from the other, and the latter two endlessly subdivided into church bodies that politely compete with one another for members. What the world does not see in the all-too-visible disunity of the churches is a sign of the unity of the Father and the Son. Church division obscures the gospel, rendering the good news less accessible to the world. Bruce Marshall puts the matter starkly:

> The credibility of the gospel—of the message that the triune God gives his own eternal life to the world in the missions of the Son and Spirit—depends upon the unity of the church by which that life is exhibited to the world. . . . The unity of the church is a necessary condition for holding the gospel true.[17]

Because the disunity of the church calls into question the trustworthiness of the gospel, the ecumenical imperative is closely aligned with the church's evangelistic imperative. The goal is not for separated churches to create a "superchurch" institution or to suppress all diversity by imposing ecclesial uniformity. Instead, for the sake of the gospel and for the well-being of the world, the churches are called to discover deep and abiding forms of recognizable Christian unity in faith, sacraments, ministry, and mission. Protestant churches emerged from the *protestari* imperative to profess, to openly proclaim the gospel. Reclaiming the founding Protestant vision leads to restoration of the unity of the whole church.

1. Luther Blissett, Q (Orlando, FL: Harcourt, 2000), p. 405.
2. Calvin, "Letter to Cranmer" (1552), in *John Calvin: Tracts and Letters*, ed. Jules Bonnet, trans. David Constable, vol. 5 (Edinburgh, UK: The Banner of Truth Trust, 1858/2009), pp. 347ff.
3. Calvin, "Letter to the reformed churches of France" (1560), in *John Calvin: Tracts and Letters*, vol. 7, pp. 80–87.
4. Confession of 1967, *Book of Confessions*, 9.27.
5. Calvin, *Institutes*, 1.14.1., pp. 160–161.
6. Confession of 1967, *Book of Confessions*, 9.27.
7. Westminster Confession of Faith, *Book of Confessions*, 6.006.
8. Buechner, *Wishful Thinking*, p. 12.
9. Luther, "The Freedom of a Christian," in *Martin Luther's Basic Theological Writings*, ed. Timothy F. Lull (Minneapolis: Fortress Press, 1989), p. 601.
10. Luther, "The Pagan Servitude of the Church," in *Martin Luther: Selections from His Writings*, ed. John Dillenberger (Garden City: Anchor, 1961), p. 345.
11. Luther, "An Appeal to the Ruling Class," in *Martin Luther: Selections*, p. 414.
12. *Book of Order*, G-1.0301a.
13. Augustine, "Confessions," in *Augustine: Confessions and Enchiridion*, ed. and trans. Albert C. Outler (Philadelphia: The Westminster Press), 6.3, p. 116.
14. Paul Tillich, *Systematic Theology*, vol. 3 (Chicago: University of Chicago Press, 1963), p. 6, passim.
15. "Sadoleto's Letter to the Genevans," in *A Reformation Debate*, ed. John C. Olin (New York: Fordham University Press, 2000), p. 40.
16. "Calvin's Reply to Sadoleto," in *A Reformation Debate*, p. 87.
17. Bruce Marshall, "The Disunity of the Church and the Credibility of the Gospel," *Theology Today 50*, no. 1 (April 1993): p. 82.

6

Reformed Accents

Worldliness to a reared Calvinist is not a vague entity but a specifiable sin of a higher order. The privilege of predestination, of being one of the Elect, carried with it the command to "come out from among them and be separate." It is only in light of my long incarceration within that principle under conditions of immigrant inferiority that my drive to reverse the order and get out there and be one of them can be at all understood.

Peter DeVries, *The Blood of the Lamb*[1]

The Reformed tradition and the churches that embody that tradition share in the faith of the one holy catholic apostolic church. They also share Protestant emphases on Scripture, justification, and the ministry of the whole people of God. Within these commonalities, Reformed churches represent some distinctive perspectives on Christian faith and life. These perspectives, derived from readings of Scripture, lead Reformed churches to shared emphases in theology, worship, church life, and ethics. The Reformed tradition is not monolithic and Reformed churches are not uniform, but the tradition and the churches that identify with it embody three overarching themes that characterize Reformed thought and life: grace, the sovereignty of God, and the character of the Christian community. While these themes are not unique to the Reformed tradition, they receive identifiable stress and characteristic expression in Reformed faith and life. The three themes are apparent in the Presbyterian Church (U.S.A.)'s Confession of 1967 and A Brief Statement of Faith. Both confessions are Trinitarian in structure, but with a twist. Rather than following the familiar pattern of the Nicene Creed and Apostles' Creed—God the Father, God the Son, and God the Holy Spirit— they follow the order of the "apostolic benediction" in 2 Corinthians 13:13: "The grace of the Lord Jesus Christ, the love of God, and the communion of the Holy Spirit be with all of you." The confessional use of this scriptural expression gives appropriate expression to Reformed emphases in Christian faith by emphasizing grace, sovereignty, and community within a rich Trinitarian perspective. Recalling the opening of the Heidelberg Catechism, A Brief Statement of Faith begins,

> In life and in death we belong to God.
>   Through the grace of our Lord Jesus Christ,
>   the love of God,
>   and the communion of the Holy Spirit,
>   we trust in the one triune God, the Holy One of Israel,
>   whom alone we worship and serve.[2]

The Grace of the Lord Jesus Christ

Like many churchly terms, *grace* is heard regularly in sermons, prayers, and hymns, but it is not always accompanied by a clear understanding of what it means. We sense that it is a good word, having something to do with God's favor, yet it may seem abstract and remote from real life. Is grace a *substance*, a religious commodity that we receive from God? Is it a *characteristic*, a spiritual capacity that God bestows on different people in varying quantities? Is grace a *force*, providing us with an impetus to holiness?

Although there have been times in the church's history when people have spoken of grace as a particular benefit measured out to us by God, Christians have more often understood that "grace" is a shorthand way of referring to the fullness of the relationship that God creates with people. What does God have to do with us, and what is the character of God's bond with the world? Is God detached from happenings in the world and aloof from our lives? Does God watch our every move, ready to judge and punish our sins? Or does God love us just the way we are, indulging our foibles and failings? Is God ready to intervene in our lives whenever we ask for something good? The answer to the abstract questions about the relationship between God and ourselves is found in the actuality of Jesus Christ. When we say "the grace of the Lord Jesus Christ," we affirm that God's Way in the world is expressed and known in Jesus Christ as God's free, faithful movement toward us in love. We do not have to settle for intangible definitions of grace, for we have before us narratives of grace, told in the familiar contours of a human life. The opening of the Gospel according to John expresses this central truth in a few flowing words that embody evangelical truth.

> And the Word became flesh
>   and dwelt among us,
>   full of grace and truth;
>   we have beheld his glory,
>   glory as of the only Son from the Father. . . .
>   And from his fullness have we all received,
>   grace upon grace (John 1:14, 16, RSV).

The Nicene Creed, the first great ecumenical statement of the church's faith, boldly professes that God's gracious self-giving is made tangible in Christ, and that it is all for the sake of human wholeness. The creed's great declarations of incarnation, atonement, crucifixion, resurrection, and ascension are not abstract doctrines, but summaries of the biblical accounts that are good news *for us*. The second major section of the Nicene Creed affirms faith in the one Lord Jesus Christ in two distinct movements: a movement that confesses the full divinity of the Son of God, and a movement that narrates the incarnation of Jesus Christ, the Human One. (Incarnation is not limited to Jesus' birth; his becoming human encompasses the whole of life, death, resurrection, ascension, and coming again.) The pivot that links the two movements is the very good news that it is all "for us and for our salvation."

> We believe in one Lord, Jesus Christ,
>   the only Son of God,
>   eternally begotten of the Father,
>   God from God, Light from Light,
>   true God from true God,
>   begotten not made,
>   of one Being with the Father;
>   through him all things were made.
> **FOR US AND FOR OUR SALVATION**
>   he came down from heaven,
>   was incarnate of the Holy Spirit and the Virgin Mary
>   and became truly human.
>   For our sake he was crucified under Pontius Pilate;
>   he suffered death and was buried.
>   On the third day he rose again
>   in accordance with the Scriptures;
>   he ascended into heaven
>   and is seated at the right hand of the Father.
>   He will come again in glory to judge the living and the dead,
>   and his kingdom will have no end.[3]

Our salvation hinges on the reality that the Son of God is "God from God, Light from Light, true God from true God, begotten not made, of one Being with the Father" *and* that "he came down from heaven" and "was incarnate of the Holy Spirit and the Virgin Mary and became truly human." A Jesus Christ less than truly God or less than truly human could not have accomplished our salvation, would not have been "for us." A century after the Nicene Creed, the ecumenical

Council of Chalcedon made the point even more forcefully: Jesus Christ is "perfect in divinity and perfect in humanity, truly God and truly human, *of one Being* with the Father as regards his divinity and *of one Being* with us as regards his humanity." Then, together with the Council of Nicaea, Chalcedon declares that this is "for us and our salvation."

Jesus Christ is truly God to us and truly human to God. As one with us and for us, Jesus Christ lived God's Way in the world fully, loving God and loving people with heart, soul, mind, and strength. His full love of God and full love of people are more than an example that we must strive to emulate. The love of God in Jesus Christ *does something* for us. As the Word became flesh, uniting God with us, so, in Christ, we are united to God. The incarnation is the union of the Word with us that brings about our union with Christ, so that we are united with him in his fulfillment of God's Way in the world—loving God completely and loving others as himself. God overcomes our self-imposed distance, for as God's Son becomes one with us and we are made one with him, we who are in Christ can now love the Lord our God with all our heart, soul, mind, and strength. God overcomes our self-imposed distance from others, for as God's Son becomes brother to all, we who are made one with him can now love our neighbors, even strangers and enemies, as ourselves.

The grace of the Lord Jesus Christ is at the center of our knowledge of God and our experience of God. The life, death, and resurrection of Jesus—and our own experience of Christ's presence—confirm that we are not loved because we deserve to be loved. The grace of the Lord Jesus Christ is known most dramatically "in that while we still were sinners Christ died for us" (Romans 5:8). That is not all. Paul goes on to say, "If while we were enemies, we were reconciled to God through the death of his Son, much more surely, having been reconciled, will we be saved by his life" (v. 11). In Christ, we know God as the One who takes the initiative to move toward us openly, freely, lovingly, unconditionally. Karl Barth speaks of God's grace in Jesus Christ as

> the demonstration, the overflowing of the love which is the being of God . . . It is love in the form of the deepest condescension. It occurs even when there is no question or claim of merit on the part of the other.[4]

To speak of grace is to speak of the freedom of the Lover who does not require that the beloved meet certain conditions: "In this is love, not that we loved God but that he loved us and sent his Son," says John (1 John 4:10).

Did the incarnate Son of God become one with only the best of humankind?

No. Scripture assures us that Christ Jesus, "being in very nature God, did not consider equality with God something to be used to his own advantage; rather, he made himself nothing by taking the very nature of a servant, being made in human likeness" (Philippians 2:6-7, TNIV).

Does Jesus parcel out love only to people good enough to deserve it?

No. Jesus says, "It is not the healthy who need a doctor, but the sick. I have not come to call the righteous, but sinners" (Mark 2:17, TNIV).

Did Jesus die on the cross only for people worthy of his sacrifice?

No. Paul says, "You see, at just the right time, when we were still powerless, Christ died for the ungodly" (Romans 5:6, TNIV).

Was Jesus raised from death only on behalf of people wise enough to appreciate his triumph?

No. Scripture proclaims, "It is by grace you have been saved, through faith— and this is not from yourselves, it is the gift of God—not by works, so that no one can boast" (Ephesians 2:8-9, TNIV).

Does the risen and ascended Christ care only for those of us who are always faithful?

No. Scripture assures us that "we have a great high priest who has ascended into heaven, Jesus the Son of God" and that "we do not have a high priest who is unable to empathize with our weaknesses, but we have one who has been tempted in every way, just as we are—yet he did not sin. Let us then approach God's throne of grace with confidence, so that we may receive mercy and find grace to help us in our time of need" (Hebrews 4:14-16, TNIV).

All Christians agree that God's love for us through the grace of Jesus Christ creates a new reality for human life: "For by grace you have been saved through faith" (Ephesians 2:8). However, some Christians stress the grace of Christ while others emphasize the human response of faith. Put another way, some concentrate on the gift that is given while others focus on the necessity of receiving the gift. The Reformed tradition comes down firmly on the side of grace, confessing that God's free gift even creates our capacity for faith and elicits faith itself. The grace of Jesus Christ is not a potential reality, requiring human faith to become effective. If we were to claim that our faith is necessary to bring about the new relationship between God and us—our salvation—then salvation would be our accomplishment—in Reformation terms, our "work." This would create for us the problem that comes with all forms of works righteousness: How could we ever be sure that our faith is good enough, true enough, faithful enough? The Reformed tradition proclaims that the distance between God and humankind is bridged by God alone, and that we are set free from constant striving to achieve sufficient faith to bridge the gap.

The Reformed tradition speaks of the free grace of Christ as "election." God's election is never to privilege. Letty Russell states, "The doctrine of election points to the need for identity as human beings in the world. Those who are nobody affirm their own self-worth as children of God by claiming that God has chosen them and enabled them to live faithfully. In this sense, to be chosen of God is to be granted full human identity and worth as a gift of God's love."[5] The Reformed emphasis on Christ's grace is liberating, setting us free from anxiety about the adequacy of our lives and the depth of our belief. Neither our works nor our faith can save us; neither is a necessary precondition to God's love. Instead, both our faith and our works are expressions of gratitude for amazing grace. Our gratitude is expressed in more than thoughts and feelings, for as we are liberated for thankful response to God's unrestricted love, we are also freed for gracious relationships with other people. As men and women who know the grace of the Lord Jesus Christ, we no longer need to make calculations about the worth, power, or ability of other people as a precondition for our love. We, too, can live grace-filled lives as we, too, love all people freely and unreservedly.

The grace of the Lord Jesus Christ, not our faith, determines the relationship between God and ourselves. Yet the Reformed emphasis upon grace does not diminish our faith. Calvin devotes fifty pages of the *Institutes* to an exploration of the meaning and significance of faith. His brief definition of faith only hints at the depth of its meaning: "Now we shall possess a right definition of faith if we call it a firm and certain knowledge of God's benevolence toward us, founded upon the truth of the freely given promise in Christ, both revealed to our minds and sealed upon our hearts through the Holy Spirit."[6] Our faith is not simply belief, but "a firm and certain knowledge" that both believes and trusts in God's goodness, leading to the fidelity of our lives. Our tendency to restrict "faith" to "belief" is an unfortunate consequence of a limitation in the English language. The Greek word translated "faith"—*pistis*—has a verb form—*pisteuo*—while the English language does not. Because we cannot translate the Greek verb as "faithing" (I faith, you faith, he/she/it faiths), it is usually rendered in English as "believing" (I believe, you believe, he/she/it believes). The result is that faith's trust and loyalty can become eclipsed by faith's belief.

"Faithing" God is *believing* that "the Word became flesh and lived among us" (John 1:14), *trusting* that from Christ "we have all received . . . grace upon grace" (v. 16), and *being loyal* to "the Lamb of God who takes away the sin of the world" (v. 29). Reformed concern for the truth about God is more than a fascination with intellectual orthodoxy. What we "faith" about the grace of the Lord Jesus Christ shapes how we understand God's Way in the world, whether we can trust that Way to be good, and how we live our way in the world in loyalty to the One who has placed us on his Way.

The Love of God

The Westminster Confession of Faith, a seventeenth-century English creed, declares that God "is the alone fountain of all being, of whom, through whom, and to whom, are all things; and hath most sovereign dominion over them, to do by them, for them, or upon them, whatsoever himself pleaseth."[7] Archaic language and an austere description of God's relationship to the world add up, in their own way, to an expression of the Reformed emphasis on the sovereignty of God—the affirmation that God is the free and powerful source of all that is. Westminster's words do not add up to the gospel's full affirmation of God's dominion over creation.

Few of us would deny God's freedom and power, but few of us would use Westminster's abstract, dispassionate descriptions of a distant deity, for they do not adequately express the richness of God's dynamic freedom as we know it in Jesus Christ. Something seems to be missing, and that something is the *love* of God. Apart from God's love, notions of absolute freedom and power are frightening. Calvin notes that "it will not suffice simply to hold that there is One whom all ought to honor and adore, unless we are also persuaded that he is the fountain of every good."[8]

If we divorce notions of God's sovereign power from Jesus Christ, we end up with silly speculation (if God is all-powerful, can God make a rock so heavy that he cannot lift it?), or fatalism (human effort is pointless because God has determined everything), or despair (God's power does not deal with human suffering). We avoid theoretical conjecture when we know God through God's self-revelation in the life, death, and resurrection of Jesus Christ. Then we can seek to understand God's sovereign power, not through dictionary definitions of omnipotence, but in Jesus Christ. What do we find when we seek? We find Christ crucified, and this rejected and executed one is "the power of God and the wisdom of God" (1 Corinthians 1:24). Power and wisdom look different in the form of a cross.

In Jesus Christ, the power of God, we do not experience God's sovereignty as compulsion. God is not a dictator, not even a benign despot. In Jesus Christ, we know the God whose power is that of One who loves, seeks, calls, and saves. God does not have a monopoly on power, fashioning the world and all within it as pawns in a divine game, moved around the board according to a mysterious heavenly strategy. Neither do we humans hold all the power, reducing God to a beggar at the door. The Lord proclaims,

For as the rain and the snow come down from heaven,
  and do not return there until they have watered the earth,
making it bring forth and sprout,
  giving seed to the sower and bread to the eater,
so shall my word be that goes out from my mouth;
  it shall not return to me empty,
but it shall accomplish that which I purpose,
  and succeed in the thing for which I sent it.
—Isaiah 55:10–11

The word of God is not simply a proposal, but a creative declaration that shapes reality. In the beginning, God speaks and the world comes to be: "God said . . . and there was" (Genesis 1). When the prophets announced "the word of the Lord," judgment occurred and hope was fulfilled (e.g., Amos 1:2; Isaiah 40:1). When the Word became flesh, the glory of the Lord was revealed (John 1:14). God's word is not an empty word, for it fulfills God's purpose in the world.

The church's confession of faith in "God the Father Almighty, creator of heaven and earth" is far more than the postulation of intelligent design that brought the universe into being. Because the Creator is the God we know in Jesus Christ, we understand that the Creator continues to love and care for all creation. As Calvin puts it, "To make God a momentary Creator who once for all finished his work, would be cold and barren . . . we see the presence of divine power shining as much in the continuing state of the universe as in its inception."[9] God's providential care for creation is the love of God in Christ: "For in [Christ] all the fullness of God was pleased to dwell, and through him God was pleased to reconcile to himself all things, whether on earth or in heaven, by making peace through the blood of his cross" (Colossians 1:19–20).

Because the Creator of the cosmos is the Redeemer and Sustainer of the cosmos, God's sovereign power is God's sovereign love. "The power of God is essentially the power of redemption," says Wendy Farley. "The power and will to redeem are more aptly symbolized by love than by models of domination, judgment or control." The issue is not one of abstract symbols or models, for "divine power is most clearly and poignantly seen in the Messiah, whose teachings, death, and resurrection manifest the love of God 'made flesh' in history."[10] Jesus Christ, the power of God, cries out to us, "Jerusalem, Jerusalem, the city that kills the prophets and stones those who are sent to it! How often have I desired to gather your children together as a hen gathers her brood under her wings, and you were not willing" (Matthew 23:37). The desire of God, beckoning in love, displays divine power more forcefully than any speculative conception of power. The Reformed tradition's emphasis on the sovereignty of God does not extol divine domination, but rather leads us to stand in awe before God's reign of love in Jesus Christ.

The sovereignty of God is the love of God for the whole created order. Abraham Kuyper, a Dutch Reformed theologian, journalist, and prime minister of the Netherlands, expressed dramatically the Reformed understanding of God's sovereignty over all of life: "There is not a square inch in the whole domain of our human existence over which Christ, who is sovereign over all, does not cry: 'Mine!' "[11] God is sovereign over all creation, so that no part of life lies outside of his nourishment and care. While "separation of church and state" is an axiom of American political life, this does not mean that Christian faith and life are confined to a spiritual ghetto. Human divisions between the "religious" and the "secular" are illusory; God is not concerned only with so-called spiritual matters, while remaining indifferent to social patterns of racial bigotry, class inequity, abuses of political power, global warming, and market-driven consumerism. The Confession of 1967 declares:

> God's redeeming work in Jesus Christ embraces the whole of human life: social and cultural, economic and political, scientific and technological, individual and corporate. It includes the natural environment as exploited and despoiled by sin. It is the will of God that the divine purpose for human life shall be fulfilled under the rule of Christ and all evil be banished from creation.[12]

Reformed insistence that the sovereign love of God knows no bounds is not a modern innovation. "Our Song of Hope" in the twentieth century and Abraham Kuyper in the nineteenth century stand in a long line of Reformed affirmations. In the eighteenth century, Jonathan Edwards Jr. criticized the recently adopted constitution of the United States for allowing the continuation of slavery. "Africans are by nature equally entitled to freedom as we are," he said. "They have the same right to their freedom which they have to their property or to their lives. Therefore, to enslave them is as really and in the same sense wrong, as to steal from them, or to rob or murder them."[13] In the seventeenth century, the Westminster Larger Catechism detailed long lists of the duties required and the sins forbidden by the eighth commandment, "Thou shalt not steal." Among the positive actions that the commandment requires are "justice in contracts and commerce . . . rendering to everyone his due . . . giving and lending freely . . . avoiding unnecessary lawsuits . . . and an endeavor by all just and lawful means to procure, preserve, and further the wealth and outward estate of others, as well as our own."[14] In the sixteenth century, Calvin asserted that the kingdom of God "does not lead us to consider the whole nature of government a thing polluted, which has nothing to do with

Christian men."[15] Calvin's thought and action on seemingly mundane matters such as economic justice, health care, education, and the environment have shaped Reformed thought and action through the centuries. Elsie McKee notes that in the Reformed tradition's gratitude and reverence for the sovereign God, "God always comes first, but the honor owed to God is often most clearly manifested in how believers live their day-to-day vocations."[16]

The Communion of the Holy Spirit

Christians within the Reformed tradition have always understood that faith is not the private possession of individuals, but is lived out by persons in community. The Christian community—the church—is a fellowship of women and men called to live together within the grace of the Lord Jesus Christ, the love of God, and the communion of the Holy Spirit. It is not simply a voluntary organization of like-minded people who gather for mutual comfort and inspiration. The community of faith is called by Christ and lives in Christ: "Where two or three are gathered in my name, I am there among them" (Matthew 18:20) is Christ's declaration that the normal form of the relationship between the triune God and us is between the triune God and us *in community.*

"Our World Belongs to God," a contemporary testimony of the Christian Reformed Church, gives graceful expression to faith in God's gift of new community:

> At Pentecost, promises old and new are fulfilled.
> The ascended Jesus becomes the baptizer,
> drenching his followers with his Spirit,
> creating a new community
> where Father, Son, and Holy Spirit make their home.
> Renewed and filled with the breath of God,
> women and men,
> young and old,
> dream dreams
> and see visions.[17]

As the new community "where Father, Son, and Holy Spirit make their home," the church is called to embody God's new Way of living in the world. When we confess the Apostles' Creed, saying, "I believe in the Holy Spirit, the holy catholic church, the communion of saints, the forgiveness of sins, the resurrection of the body, and the life everlasting," we are not merely affirming a laundry list of unrelated doctrinal leftovers. Just as our confession of faith in God the Father and Jesus Christ is followed by narrative depictions of these movements of God among us, so the third article of the Apostles' Creed narrates the presence of the Holy Spirit in our midst. God's presence among us as Holy Spirit is the divine mission of establishing and sustaining the reality of human communion with God and with other people. Called together by the gracious love of God in Jesus Christ, the church is a communion enduring through time and space in which God's forgiveness generates mutual forgiveness, and God's faithfulness secures certain hope.

In the presence of the Holy Spirit, the church is called to be *holy*, a distinctive, Spirit-shaped community in the world. The church's response to the Spirit's presence is always ambiguous; efforts to live as a new people are mixed with grand and petty conformities to the culture. Any church may be little different from other organizations in society, but in spite of obvious assimilation by the culture and accommodation to society's values, the Spirit remains present as the movement of God to create a new and different human community in the world.

In the presence of the Holy Spirit, the church is called to be *catholic*, rising above the limitations of race, gender, class, and nation, and overcoming every division of faith and practice, so that the community is whole. Again, the church's response is ambiguous; some dividing walls are broken down while others are reinforced. Any church may be captive to exclusivist structures and divisive assertions of faith and life, but, in spite of self-imposed restrictions, the Spirit is God's presence among us to create a new space of freedom in the world.

In the presence of the Holy Spirit, the church is called to be a community of forgiven people (*the communion of saints*) who live together in mutual forgiveness (*the forgiveness of sins*). The church is called to live now in anticipation of the final victory over sin and death (*the resurrection of the body*). The church is called to move beyond "the way things are" toward God's Way in the world (*the life everlasting*). Even as we speak the words of the creed, we know that for every sign of faithfulness there seems to be evidence of crass conformity to the prevailing spirit of the age. The church is a community of ordinary people, plainly guilty of the charge of hypocrisy; what we claim in our creeds falls far short of what we display in our life together.

The Reformed tradition does not make unrealistic claims for the character of Christian community, as if the church were divine, floating above the real world. Neither does the tradition fall into cynical dismissal of Christian community, as if the church were a mere organization, fully immersed in the real world. Dutch theologian G. C. Berkouwer expresses Reformed realism by noting: "The *credo ecclesiam* does not direct our attention only to what ought to be and what ought to happen, but to what obviously has happened in the lives of [Christians]."[18] What has happened in Christian communities is a mix of faithfulness and infidelity, truth and falsehood, obedience and defiance, love and indifference . . . the list goes on. Yet the Spirit remains present, the call continues to be heard, and men and women continue to respond. The Reformed tradition provides us with two resources for faithful discipleship: utter realism about the church and utter trust in the presence of the Holy Spirit. Honesty and hope are the twin pillars that support Reformed community.

The Reformed tradition's utter realism about the church and its confidence in the presence of the Holy Spirit lead to the conviction that the church's ministry and mission are the calling of the whole people of God. In the Reformed tradition, ministry is not the domain of a particular group of people called "clergy," who lead a larger group called "laity." This un-Reformed clergy/laity distinction obscures the reality that all specific ministries of the church are particular expressions of the ministry of the whole body of Christ. All Christians are gifted for ministry, and so there is a real sense in which all are ordained to ministry in their baptisms. This leads Reformed churches to establish organizational structures that engage the whole people of God. Within this foundational ministry of the whole people of God, persons may be called to perform specific functions that are important to the life of particular communities of faith. Church school teachers, choir members, treasurers, cooks, ushers and greeters, gardeners, and others are called formally and informally, and exercise their gifts on behalf of the whole congregation.

Some ministries are considered *necessary* to the spiritual health and faithful life of *every* Christian community. The whole church gives order to these necessary functions by regularizing their shape, their duties, their qualifications, and their approval. These "ordered ministries," and the persons who are called to them, are grounded in baptism and established in ordination—the whole church's act of setting apart for particular service.

Following Calvin, the mainstream of Reformed ecclesiology recognizes three ordered ministries: deacon, elder, and minister. These three ministries represent two ecclesial functions: ministries of the Word and Sacrament performed by presbyters (pastors and elders) and ministries of service performed by deacons. These ministries are collegial and exercised in community, through councils (sessions/consistories, presbyteries/classes, and general assemblies/synods). No minister, elder, or deacon is self-sufficient and no ministry is exercised apart from the other ministries or in isolation from the whole people of God. The structures of Reformed church order are designed to ensure that ordinary people are chosen by ordinary communities in the confidence that "through the ministers whom [God] has entrusted this office and conferred the grace to carry it out, he dispenses and distributes his gifts to the church; and he shows himself as present by manifesting the power of his Spirit in this institution, that it not be vain or idle."[19]

Although Reformed churches have sometimes placed too much confidence in structures, the Reformed tradition's intention has always been to shape Christian community in patterns of grace, love, and communion. The sixteenth-century confession of the Reformed churches "dispersed in France" expresses this intention clearly:

We believe that the [true church] ought to be governed in accordance with the order established by our Lord Jesus Christ, having pastors, elders, and deacons. In this way, pure doctrine can be maintained, vices can be corrected and suppressed, the poor and afflicted can be helped in their need, assemblies can be gathered in the name of God, and both great and small can be edified.[20]

Jürgen Moltmann gives more contemporary expression to the character of Reformed community through the concept of friendship. He says that the communion of saints, the community of faith and faithfulness, "is really the fellowship of friends who live in the friendship of Jesus and spread friendliness in the fellowship, by meeting the forsaken with affection and the despised with respect."[21] Reformed Christians strive to make this more than a lofty sentiment by shaping church life in ways that are open to all, both within and outside of the community of faith, by remaining open to the presence of the Holy Spirit.

"The grace of the Lord Jesus Christ, the love of God, and the communion of the Holy Spirit" are not simply the words of a benediction or a statement of faith; they are the reality in which we live and move and have our being.

1. Peter DeVries, *The Blood of the Lamb* (Boston: Little, Brown and Company, 1961), p. 45.
2. A Brief Statement of Faith, *Book of Confessions*, 10.1, p. 267.
3. Nicene Creed, *Book of Confessions*, 1.2, p. 3.
4. Barth, *Church Dogmatics*, II.2, pp. 9ff.
5. Russell, *The Church in the Round* (Louisville: Westminster John Knox Press, 1993), p. 169.
6. *Institutes*, 3.2.7., p. 551.
7. Westminster Confession of Faith, *Book of Confessions*, 6.012, p. 124.
8. *Institutes*, 1.2.1., p. 40.
9. Ibid., 1.16.1., p. 197.
10. Wendy Farley, *Tragic Vision and Divine Compassion* (Louisville: Westminster/John Knox Press, 1990), p. 100.
11. Abraham Kuyper, "Sphere Sovereignty," in *Abraham Kuyper: A Centennial Reader*, ed. James D. Bratt (Grand Rapids: Eerdmans, 1998), p. 488.
12. Confession of 1967, Inclusive Language Text, 9.53.
13. Jonathan Edwards Jr., "The Injustice and Impolicy of the Slave Trade, and of Slavery," in *Reformed Reader*, ed. William Stacey Johnson and John Leith, vol. 1 (Louisville: Westminster/John Knox Press, 1993), p. 371.
14. Westminster Larger Catechism, *Book of Confessions*, 7.251, p. 218.
15. *Institutes*, 4.20.2., p. 1487.
16. Elsie Anne McKee, "Calvin's Teaching on Social and Economic Issues," in *John Calvin Rediscovered: The Impact of His Social and Economic Thought*, ed. Edward Dommen and James Bratt (Louisville: Westminster John Knox Press, 2007), p. 21.
17. "Our World Belongs to God: A Contemporary Testimony" (Grand Rapids: Christian Reformed Church in North America, 2008), paragraph 28.
18. G. C. Berkouwer, *Studies in Dogmatics: The Church* (Grand Rapids: Eerdmans, 1976), p. 9.
19. *Institutes*, 4.3.2., p. 1055.
20. *The French Confession of 1559*, trans. Ellen Babinsky and Joseph D. Small (Louisville: Office of Theology and Worship, 1998), XXIX, p. 14.
21. Jürgen Moltmann, *The Church in the Power of the Spirit* (New York: Harper & Row, 1977), p. 316.

Gratitude in an Age of Achievement

7

Surely God knew by now that they offered up sentence prayers every morning. He must know what they were going to say, even, since most of them just repeated what they'd said other mornings. The girls said thank-yous—"Thank you for the trees and flowers" and such. . . . The boys were more likely to make requests. "Let the Orioles win tonight" was commonest. ("If it be Thy will," Sister Myra always added in a hurry.) The only exception was Dermott Kyle, who said, "Thank you for air-conditioning." That always got a laugh. Thomas usually asked for good swimming weather, but today he prayed for Kenny Larson's earache to go away. For one thing, Kenny was his best friend. Also Thomas liked to come up with some different sentence now and then, and this one made Sister Myra nod approvingly.

Sister Audrey offered the closing sentence. "Dear God," she said, "look down upon us and understand us, we humbly beg in Jesus' name. Amen."

Anne Tyler, Saint Maybe[1]

Question: What is the fourth petition [of the Lord's Prayer]?
Answer: "Give us this day our daily bread." That is: be pleased to provide for all our bodily needs so that thereby we may acknowledge that thou art the only source of all that is good, and that without thy blessing neither our care and labor nor thy gifts can do us any good. Therefore, may we withdraw our trust from all creatures and place it in thee alone.[2]

The answer seems remote, not only because it comes from a centuries-old catechism, but also because it is not clear to us that God is the *only* source of *all* that is good in our lives. In fact, most North Americans take for granted that the good in our lives comes from our own efforts and achievements.

Every autumn is brought to a close by Thanksgiving Day. As we sit down to a feast, we do not thank God for the provision of food that will sustain the nation through the coming winter, or for everyone's shelter from the stormy blast. Our oddly abstract gratitude is largely confined to the blessings enjoyed by our own families, often with undertones of satisfaction that we have many of the good things of life that others lack. What makes the Thanksgiving holiday so ambiguous is that while we know we are supposed to thank God for what we have, we really believe that our "blessings" are the result of our own efforts. Our work, our management of financial resources, and our planning yield the bounty we pause to appreciate. On the face of it, our gratitude for what *we* have achieved is reasonable enough. Our hard work does earn our daily bread and provide all the things that make life secure. If we enjoy the good things of life, it is because we have toiled to provide them for our families and us. Even good health is, at least in part, a matter of our own doing. If we stop smoking, watch our cholesterol count, and exercise regularly, won't we make ourselves healthier and happier?

We live in a society that values *self*-reliance. Yet, distressingly, we know that many people within our society cannot rely on themselves to provide daily bread or any of the other necessities of life. Homelessness and hunger are realities in American cities, not just in Calcutta or Mogadishu. Even if our reliance on ourselves is sufficient, there are many for whom self-reliance is not enough to produce a Norman Rockwell scene on the fourth Thursday in November. Where, we may wonder, is God, when so many people throughout the world have so little to be thankful for? And where, we may wonder, is God, when so many others thank only *themselves* for the material splendors they enjoy?

It may be that our perplexity about gratitude to God grows out of the dominant American image of the Pilgrims' "first Thanksgiving." The scene of a community feast to celebrate a successful harvest has conditioned us to equate gratitude with the presence of food, clothes, shelter, and other basics of life. Yet, it is precisely these things that now seem less God-given and more our own taken-for-granted assets. We harvest our food in twenty-four-hour supermarkets or in restaurants, weave our wardrobes from an array of stores in the mall, and construct shelter that includes air conditioning and a television set in every room. Does God provide us with all those things? Should we thank God as we download music into our newest iPod or microwave the evening meal?

Living Thanksgiving

> *Question:* What is your only comfort, in life and in death?
> *Answer:* That I belong—body and soul, in life and in death—not to myself but to my faithful Savior, Jesus Christ . . .
> *Question:* How many things must you know that you may live and die in the blessedness of this comfort?
> *Answer:* Three. First, the greatness of my sin and wretchedness. Second, how I am freed from all my sins and their wretched consequences. Third, what gratitude I owe to God for such redemption.[3]

Like the opening words of this chapter, these questions and answers are part of the Heidelberg Catechism, a sixteenth-century exposition of the Reformed perspective on Christian faith and life. Now one of the confessional standards of the Reformed Church in America, the Christian Reformed Church, and the Presbyterian Church (U.S.A.), the Heidelberg Catechism is noted for its engaging accent on the experience of the Christian life. Nevertheless, some of its language grates on twentieth-first-century ears; sin, wretchedness, and misery are no longer our customary categories for understanding human life.

Human Misery

The Heidelberg Catechism is divided into three parts: "Of Man's Misery," "Of Man's Redemption," and "Thankfulness." Human misery, according to the catechism, is the price of "sin and its wretched consequences." Blunt talk about sin was common in the sixteenth century, but it is not an agreeable subject in twenty-first-century North America. A generation ago, the noted psychiatrist and Presbyterian elder Karl Menninger asked, "Whatever became of sin?" His book was an analysis of the disappearance of both the word and the concept of sin from American public (and church) discourse. "Why?" Menninger asks. "Doesn't anyone sin anymore? Doesn't anyone believe in sin?"[4]

It is obvious that individuals, groups, and nations commit grand and petty wrongs daily, but Menninger contends that contemporary reluctance to call them sins results from a shift in the allocation of responsibility for evil. Whatever became of sin? First, Menninger says, sin became *crime*:

> It became the civilized custom to attempt to legislate morality and to coerce virtue by law. The law took over not only the great destructive sins—murder and mayhem and rape—it took over the Ten Commandments, then it took over the lesser sins and vices.[5]

Sin became crime, the state became the enforcer of morality, and imprisonment replaced repentance. Think of the expansion of hate crimes legislation. Expressing hatred of particular ethnic groups was once sinful; now it is merely illegal. The allocation of responsibility continued as sin (and crime) became *illness*. Both immoral and criminal behavior became attributed to a vast array of syndromes that require therapy rather than imprisonment or repentance. Immorality now leads to "entering rehab" rather than the confessional, and crime leads to illness defenses rather than guilty pleas.

The disappearance of both the word and the notion of sin from American culture is accompanied by its fading away from the church's vocabulary of faith and life. Cornelius Plantinga Jr. notes,

> The awareness of sin used to be our shadow. Christians hated sin, feared it, fled from it, grieved over it. . . . But the shadow has dimmed.[6]

Plantinga observes that in contemporary culture "sin" is more often found in cartoon captions or on restaurant descriptions of chocolate desserts than in sermons.

Recognition that the concept of sin has faded from both society and church is not limited to Christian writers. Henry Fairlie, a self-described "reluctant unbeliever," is convinced that psychological explanations of the waywardness of our own behavior and sociological explanations of the evils of our societies have come to a dead end. Their major premise—"that our own faults and those of our societies are the result of some kind of mechanical failure, which has only to be diagnosed and understood for us to set it right"—does not lead to personal or social improvement.[7] Fairlie goes on to say what the contemporary church seems to have forgotten:

> If we do not take seriously our capacity for evil, we are unable to take seriously our capacity for good. Both become little more than coincidences, the results of our genes and our psychology and our environment, for which our responsibility is unclear.[8]

Mention of sin is largely absent from the church's sermons, education, and counseling. The vocabulary of sin is largely confined to the church's liturgy, and even there it is domesticated. Reformed worship has always been characterized by confession of sin (often over the objections of persons who proclaim their innocence of the prayers' enumerated offenses). Yet even when prayers of confession remain, they are softened to make them more palatable to virtuous congregations. The regular insertion of the little word *often* into prayers is a clear indication of wiggle room: "We are silent when we should speak" becomes "we are *often* silent when we should speak," thus balancing some virtue—we are not *always* silent when we should speak—with our acknowledgment of periodic lapses. Other moderations include the confession of inadequate inner dispositions rather than our actions that serve self rather than God, that wound the people we love, that participate willingly in social systems that diminish others. In many congregations that retain the liturgical form, confession of sin has become little more than an expression of mild regret that we have failed to live up to our potential.

Recovering an awareness of the reality of sin in the world, and in our own lives, is an important challenge for Reformed Christians, but it should not become a morbid preoccupation with human fault. The Heidelberg Catechism itself spends little time on "sin and its wretched consequences"—only nine out of one hundred twenty-nine questions—before moving on to the redemption God brings to human life. Its brief series of questions and answers make it clear that sin resides at the core of our lives, and that "human misery" flows from our unwillingness to fulfill the Great Commandment: "You shall love the Lord your God with all your heart, and with all your soul, and with all your mind. . . . You shall love your neighbor as yourself." Incapable of loving God truly and neighbor fully, we distance ourselves from both. Our self-imposed estrangement *is* miserable, for isolation is never splendid. Frederick Buechner provides a vivid description of the Reformed understanding of sin.

> The power of sin is centrifugal. When at work in a human life, it tends to push everything out toward the periphery. Bits and pieces go flying off until only the core is left. Eventually, bits and pieces of the core itself go flying off until in the end nothing at all is left. "The wages of sin is death" is St. Paul's way of saying the same thing.[9]

What is to be done about the reality of sin and the constricted life it produces? The Reformed tradition has always included a realistic understanding of evil and sin, and their "wretched consequences" for human life. The tradition does not stop there, wallowing in guilt and paralyzed by despair. Instead, it stresses the good news of God's gracious redemption of human life, freeing us from captivity to sin and freeing us for life in communion with God and with other people.

Redemption

The catechism does not dwell on human sin and misery, because its central concern is human redemption. What we are incapable of doing for ourselves God does for us: Our Lord Jesus Christ is freely given to us for our redemption and our righteousness. Through the grace of the Lord Jesus Christ, the love of God, and the communion of the Holy Spirit, we are freed from the bondage to sin that separates us from God and isolates us from neighbors, restoring real communion and freeing us for a life of love received and love shared.

In a lovely way, the Heidelberg Catechism accentuates the benefits that come to us in our redemption, but it never forgets that these benefits flow from God, who loves and saves us, who re-creates us for real life, who nourishes us for growth in faithfulness. The catechism's aim is to set forth the gospel, the good news of what God has done in Jesus Christ and is doing in the continuing presence of the Holy Spirit. By exploring the contours of the Apostles' Creed, the Sacraments of Baptism and the Lord's Supper, the Heidelberg Catechism helps us to understand what is true about God—who God is and what God does—so that we can we begin to understand the truth about ourselves—who we are and what we do.

Our belief in God the Father Almighty, maker of heaven and earth, is not mere assent to the proposition that God created the universe. Heidelberg invites us to trust in God's fatherly care of creation, so that we are able "to be patient in adversity, grateful in the midst of blessing, and to trust our faithful God and

Father for the future, assured that no creature shall separate us from his love."[10] Our belief in Jesus Christ is not mere remembrance of a long ago and faraway life, death, and resurrection. Heidelberg invites us to receive here and now the benefit of Christ's death and resurrection: "That by his power our old self is crucified, put to death, and buried with him" and that "we too are now raised by his power to a new life."[11] Our belief in the Holy Spirit is not mere acknowledgment of religious spirituality. Heidelberg invites us to trust that "God's Spirit is also given to me, preparing me through a true faith to share in Christ and all his benefits, that he comforts me and will abide with me forever."[12]

It is for *all of that*—for God's gracious redemption—that we can be grateful. Food, clothes, and shelter are not inconsequential, for they are part of God's good world and part of God's good will for human life. Calvin goes beyond God's provision of life's necessities to express delight in God's endowment of creation with the beauty of flowers, the pleasure of wine, the glory of color, and all the other features of this world that go beyond the strictly necessary to grant us sheer pleasure.[13] Yet these abundant blessings are not at the core of human life. Apart from the integrity of genuine communion with God and other people, our possessions and delights (or even our lack) can become markers of our distance from God and neighbors.

Thankfulness

Little wonder, then, that the Heidelberg Catechism follows its proclamation of God's grace with a concluding exploration of thankfulness. Gratitude to God for saving grace is the appropriate human response to what the Father has done through Jesus Christ in the power of the Holy Spirit. Human gratitude for the grace of God has always been a central characteristic of Reformed theology. Karl Barth gives eloquent voice to the Reformed understanding of grace and gratitude:

> Grace and gratitude belong together like heaven and earth. Grace evokes gratitude like the voice of an echo. Gratitude follows grace like thunder lightning. . . . We are speaking of the grace of God who is God for man, and of the gratitude of man as his response to this grace. . . . The two belong together, so that only gratitude can correspond to grace, and this correspondence cannot fail.[14]

The Heidelberg Catechism's insight into the shape of human thankfulness is unexpected. The catechism says nothing about feeling grateful and little about our expressions of gratitude. Instead, Heidelberg explores thankfulness as something we *do*, the defining quality of who we are and how we live.

Question: Since we are redeemed from our sin and its wretched consequences by grace through Christ without any merit of our own, why must we do good works?

Answer: Because just as Christ has redeemed us with his blood he also renews us through his Holy Spirit according to his own image, so that with our whole life we may show ourselves grateful to God for his goodness and that he may be glorified through us.[15]

The catechism's concluding section on thankfulness consists of questions and answers about the law—the Ten Commandments—and about prayer—the Lord's Prayer. The shape of human gratitude for God's grace is obedience and praise as the defining character of our whole life! Feelings of gratitude, while appropriate, are not at the heart of thanksgiving. Words of gratitude, while fitting, are insufficient. Our response to what God has done involves the whole of life and all of life's actions. If God has restored us to right relationships with God and neighbor, then our grateful response is the living of right relationships with God and neighbor.

The Law as Gift and Gratitude

It seems odd to think of the law as a joyful expression of thanksgiving. Countless sermons and Bible studies have conditioned us to contrast law (bad) with love (good), and to make unfavorable comparisons between Pharisees (legalists) and Christians (people of faith). At best, Christian obedience to the law may be seen as a duty, but the law's requirements are rarely thought of as a principal form of thanksgiving to God. Yet the Reformed tradition, while fully aware that law may deceive and oppress people, acknowledges the fundamentally positive role of God's law in the life of faith.

Calvin spelled out three uses of God's law, only two of which are familiar to most contemporary Reformed Christians.

1. The law is like a mirror that reflects our sin. "While [the law] shows God's righteousness . . . it warns, informs, convicts, and lastly condemns, every man of his own unrighteousness."[16] As the requirements of the law display the shape of righteousness that is acceptable to God, they simultaneously expose our refusal to live righteously. We do not live as the law commands. Human sin is pervasive, not confined to occasional breaking of individual commandments. In fact, periodic remorse over particular misdeeds is itself evidence of the sinful impulse to justify our lives by admitting to limited, occasional mistakes.

The law displays both the breadth of God's good will for human life and the extent of our unwillingness to embrace that life. "You shall not covet anything that is your neighbor's," proclaims the tenth commandment. Is anyone innocent of breaking this commandment? We may never have robbed, murdered, or committed adultery, but everyone among us has felt a twinge of jealousy and desired things that others have. Our entire advertising-dominated, market-driven, consumer-oriented economic system is built upon the recognition that covetousness is at the core of our being. Reformed approaches to the law are less interested in the fault that is exposed by the law than in the redeemed life that can be lived within the law.

The Westminster Larger Catechism, a seventeenth-century exposition of the Reformed perspective, sets forth positively the life God wills for us, and negatively the sin we must avoid to live within God's will:

> The duties required in the Tenth Commandment are: such a full contentment with our own condition, and such a charitable frame of the whole soul towards our neighbor, as that all our inward motions and affections touching him, tend unto and further all that good which is his. . . . The sins forbidden in the Tenth Commandment are: discontentment with our own estate; envying, and grieving at the good of our neighbor, together with all inordinate motions and affections to anything that is his.[17]

Westminster is candid about our propensity for always wanting more than what we have, but its chief concern is to direct our gaze outward, toward our neighbors and the furthering of their welfare. Grateful fulfillment of the law replaces the sin that comes between others and us with bonds of communion.

The law of God is not merely a checklist for personal morality, but the setting forth of a way of living that encompasses personal, social, political, and economic aspects of life. The law lays bare our pretensions to righteousness, and yet its purpose is not to make us feel guilty or cause us to despair, but to open us to God's grace. As the law confronts us with our failure in righteousness, it proclaims God's gracious mercy, showing us that "in Christ [God's] face shines, full of grace and gentleness, even upon us poor and unworthy sinners."[18]

2. *The law preserves public law and order.* "At least by fear of punishment," Calvin notes, the law serves "to restrain certain men who are untouched by any care for what is just and right unless compelled by hearing the dire threats of the law."[19] Societies enact laws against theft, robbery, man-stealing, and the like, setting forth punishments for lawbreakers, because they know some people will act rightly only when they fear the penalties that will come from doing wrong.

3. *The law helps us to shape our lives in love of God and neighbor.* We are familiar with the theological and social uses of law, but it is Calvin's "third use" of the law that characterizes the Reformed tradition's ethic of gratitude. "The third and principal use, which pertains more closely to the proper purpose of the law, finds its place among believers in whose hearts the Spirit of God already lives and reigns."[20] As God's good gift to a redeemed people, the law is an aid and

encouragement to life lived in God's Way, life that is meaningful and purposeful. Yes, the law uncovers human unrighteousness and leads to reliance on God's grace. Yes, the law restrains social evil by threatening punishment for criminal behavior. For Christians, people who know God's grace, the law displays God's good will for human life.

Serene Jones states that a fully formed Reformed understanding of God's law "does not look primarily like a set of abstractly asserted standards for measuring right behavior but more like an exquisite, acclaimed portrait that presents to us a vision of the godly life. The law is an aesthetic space—a portrait of a life." She goes on to say that the law has power to shape personal and community life, not through compulsion, but "because the people who accept it find that it is so beautiful they cannot help but adore it and seek to live within it."[21] Living God's good and beneficial will for beautiful human life—living God's law—is the fitting form of our gratitude for God's grace, the "thunder following the lightning." "Thanks is the one all-embracing, but as such valid and inescapable, content of the law of the covenant," says Barth. "All the laws of Israel, and all the concrete demands . . . are simply developments and specific forms of this one law, demands not to withhold from the God of the covenant the thanks which is His due, but to render it with a whole heart."[22]

In many contemporary American churches—including Reformed churches— the minister recites the Ten Commandments before the prayer of confession. This practice reflects the "first use" of the law, convicting us of our sin so that we will confess our unrighteousness. In a Reformed ordering of worship, the law comes after the prayer of confession and assurance of pardon. The law is not an accusation, but God's gift to forgiven people, displaying the shape of new life that redeemed people can live. Within the Reformed tradition, living the law is an all-embracing expression of thankfulness for God's grace, the grateful response of people in the living of real life. Moreover, the acts of gratitude bring genuine fulfillment to human life, for it is in living the law that we live within the fullness of communion with God who is now known as loving Father, and with other people who are now known as neighbors.

Prayer as Gift and Gratitude

Question: Why is prayer necessary for Christians?
Answer: Because it is the chief part of the gratitude which God requires of us.[23]

It seems fitting to think of prayer as a living expression of thanksgiving to God, for we say grace at meals and teach our children to thank God for blessings. Yet, frequent questions about "unanswered prayer" reveal that the primary understanding of prayer has more to do with asking than thanking. We may find ourselves in prayer only when we are at the end of our rope, unable to bring about the things we want. At its best, prayer that asks something of God is an expression of our confidence in God's goodness, but too often we rely on God only when we have exhausted our own resources. For some people, God is the last resort when medical treatment has failed or when life's burdens have become too heavy to bear. For others, God is little more than a vending machine: Insert the prayer and expect the product. If the machine works, they will be thankful, but if they do not receive what they have paid for they will be dismayed by unanswered prayer. Whether in deep desperation or crass acquisitiveness, people often search for the right formula, hoping that God will answer our prayers if only we can discover the right way to pray. In the end, many more people abandon prayer altogether.

Prayer is the primary form of our relationship to God, a relationship inaugurated by God's grace in Jesus Christ. Thus, the primary expression of our relationship is gratitude for that grace, thanksgiving for that presence. We do not thank God for many things, but for one thing. Even when our prayers are explicitly prayers of thanksgiving, we need not run our fingers down a list of blessings, thanking God for each item in turn. The heart of prayer is not giving thanks for multiple blessings, but for one blessing—that God is God, the God who is with and for us in Jesus Christ. If we focus our thanksgiving only on the blessings we have, what are we to do about the blessings we lack? Ask for them until our every wish has been satisfied? If we confine our gratitude to *our* blessings, what are we to do with people who are less blessed? Thank God that we are not like them? Our prayers of thanksgiving are expressions of gratitude for God's redemption of our lives, and for the fullness of life that our redemption brings.

Only when we appreciate that prayer—all prayer—is "the chief part of the gratitude which God requires of us" can we begin to understand what it means to ask when we pray. Again, we do not ask for many things, but for one thing: for God, for God's continuing, gracious presence. When we pray the Lord's Prayer, we thank God for being God, then ask God to continue being God with us and for us. We ask for God's kingdom to come, for God's Way to be the way of the world. We ask that God's will be done, in our lives and throughout the world. We ask for the bread we need, knowing that our deepest need is for "the bread of life," Jesus Christ. We ask for God's forgiveness, and for the capacity to forgive others. We ask for safety from all that leads us away from love of God and of neighbor. We ask for deliverance from evil's assaults on us and the whole world.

When we ask, not for many things, but for one thing, our petitions are no longer items on a shopping list, but a grateful acknowledgement that the presence of God for which we pray is a generous presence that invites us to make known our needs, the needs of those we know, and the needs of the world. Asking for the one thing that really matters transforms mere desire into grateful hope in the goodness of God.

When the disciples asked Jesus to teach them how to pray, he said a prayer. As we pray the Lord's Prayer, we, too, learn to pray. The primary prayer of the Christian community may help us to understand that we learn how to pray within the community of faith, in corporate worship of God. The Presbyterian Church's *Book of Common Worship* includes more than 1,200 prayers. Among these, the great prayers of thanksgiving during Baptism and the Lord's Supper are models for all our praying. The *Book of Common Worship*'s great prayers of thanksgiving always begin with a dialogue between the leader of worship and the congregation:

> The Lord be with you.
> **And also with you.**
> Let us give thanks to the Lord our God.
> **It is right to give our thanks and praise.**

The prayers then thank and praise God for all God's gracious acts in the past, present, and future, gratefully remembering Christ's work of redemption and calling upon the Holy Spirit to draw people into the presence of Christ. The prayers include intercessions for the church and the needs of the world. They conclude with praise for the triune God, followed by the Lord's Prayer. The community's faithful expressions of thanks and praise can shape our personal prayer so that it, too, becomes grateful response to the grace of God.

"We do not know how to pray as we ought," Paul says (Romans 8:26). For too many Christians, it is also accurate to say simply, "we do not pray as we ought." Christian neglect of "the chief part of gratitude" is not a uniquely modern problem. Centuries ago, it puzzled Calvin: "It is strange that by promises of such great sweetness we are affected either so coldly or hardly at all," he says, "so that many of us prefer to wander through mazes and, forsaking the fountain of living waters, to dig for ourselves dry cisterns rather than to embrace God's generosity, freely given to us."[24] There are many reasons for contemporary negligence in prayer, but one significant cause may be the decrease in singing and praying the psalms. For centuries, Reformed churches were known for the use of the psalms in worship and in family devotions, but hymns, praise music, and "free prayer" have now displaced them.

The psalms are rich resources for prayer because they give voice to both sides of the conversation of faith. People speak, and God answers; God speaks, and people answer. The psalms express praise and lament, joy and sorrow, affection and anger, hope and despair, confidence in God and dismay at God's inaction. Both personal and communal responses to God are present in full measure, so that as we pray and sing the psalms we are taught to pray in full measure.

O give thanks to the LORD, for he is good;
for his steadfast love endures forever! (Psalm 107:1, RSV)

We give thee thanks, O God, we give thee thanks;
thy name is brought very near to us
in the story of thy wonderful deeds. (Psalm 75:1, JB)

Save us, O LORD our God,
and gather us from among the nations,
that we may give thanks to thy holy name
and glory in thy praise. (Psalm 106:47, RSV)

Repent Lord, save me.
You promised; keep faith!
In death, who remembers you?
In Sheol, who gives you thanks? (Psalm 6:5, ICEL)

Deliver me from my persecutors;
for they are too strong for me!
Bring me out of prison,
that I may give thanks to thy name! (Psalm 142:6-7, RSV)

I give thee thanks, O LORD, with my whole heart;
before the gods I sing thy praise;
I bow down toward thy holy temple
and give thanks to thy name
for thy steadfast love and thy faithfulness. (Psalm 138:1-2, RSV)

"Prayer derives from what the Christian receives," says Karl Barth. "It is simply the human fulfillment of this receiving, the direct expression of the life of the one who stands amazed at what God is and does for him . . . that God is actually for him, and that God acts for him."[25] Prayer that is thanksgiving is also confession and penitence, petition and intercession, yet these elements of prayer are transformed by the fundamental characteristic of gratitude that God speaks and hears, enabling us to hear and speak.

Question: What is the meaning of the little word "Amen"?

Answer: Amen means: this shall truly and certainly be. For my prayer is much more certainly heard by God than I am persuaded in my heart that I desire such things from him.[26]

In much of the Christian life, last things are really first. The "Amen" at the end of our prayers acknowledges that we are already loved by God, joined to Christ, and living in the power of the Holy Spirit.

Grace and Gratitude

Grace evokes gratitude like the voice of an echo. The image is lovely, but we know that grace and gratitude are not ethereal specters. Just as God's grace is made down-to-earth in Jesus Christ, so gratitude becomes actual in the law and prayer, in obedience and praise. Thus, life itself becomes thanksgiving for the One who gives life and new life.

> In gratitude to God, empowered by the Spirit,
>   we strive to serve Christ in our daily tasks
>   and to live holy and joyful lives,
>   even as we watch for God's new heaven and new earth,
>   praying, "Come, Lord Jesus!"[27]

1. Anne Tyler, *Saint Maybe* (New York: Alfred A. Knopf, 1991), pp. 136ff.
2. Heidelberg Catechism, *Book of Confessions*, 4.125.
3. Ibid., 4.001–4.002.
4. Karl Menninger, *Whatever Became of Sin?* (New York: Hawthorn Books, 1973), p. 14.
5. Ibid., p. 67.
6. Cornelius Plantinga Jr., *Not the Way It's Supposed to Be: A Breviary of Sin* (Grand Rapids: Eerdmans, 1995), p. ix.
7. Henry Fairlie, *The Seven Deadly Sins Today* (Notre Dame, IN: University of Notre Dame Press, 1978), p. vii.
8. Ibid., p. 15.
9. Buechner, *Wishful Thinking*, p. 88.
10. Heidelberg Catechism, 4.028.
11. Ibid., 4.043, 4.045.
12. Ibid., 4.053.
13. *Institutes*, 3.10.2., pp. 720ff.
14. Barth, *Church Dogmatics*, IV.1., p. 41.
15. Heidelberg Catechism, 4.086.
16. *Institutes*, 2.7.6., p. 354.
17. Westminster Larger Catechism, *Book of Confessions*, 7.257–7.258.
18. *Institutes*, 2.7.8., p. 357.
19. Ibid., 2.7.10, p. 358.
20. Ibid., 2.7.12., p. 360.
21. Serene Jones, "Glorious Creation, Beautiful Law," in *Feminist and Womanist Essays in Reformed Dogmatics*, ed. Amy Plantinga Pauw and Serene Jones (Louisville: Westminster John Knox Press, 2006), pp. 33ff.
22. Barth, *Church Dogmatics*, IV.1., p. 42.
23. Heidelberg Catechism, 4.116.
24. *Institutes*, 3.20.14., p. 867.
25. Barth, *Church Dogmatics*, III.3., pp. 270ff.
26. Heidelberg Catechism, 4.129.
27. *A Brief Statement of Faith*, 10.4.

8

Worship in an Age of Self-Fulfillment

Nothing so inevitably blackened my heart as an obligatory Sunday at the Shadyside Presbyterian Church: the minister's Britishy accent; the putative hypocrisy of my parents, who forced me to go, though they did not; the putative hypocrisy of the expensive men and women who did go. I knew enough of the Bible to damn these people to hell, citing chapter and verse. My house shall be called a house of prayer; but ye have made it a den of thieves. . . .

It was the first Sunday of the month, I remembered, shocked. Today was Communion. I would have to sit through Communion, with its two species, embarrassment and tedium. . . . I had successfully avoided Communion for years.

Annie Dillard, *An American Childhood*[1]

The Presbyterian Directory for Worship begins with the ringing claim: "Christian worship joyfully ascribes all praise and honor, glory and power to the triune God. In worship the people of God acknowledge God present in the world and in their lives. As they respond to God's claim and redemptive action in Jesus Christ, believers are transformed and renewed. In worship the faithful offer themselves to God and are equipped for God's service in the world."[2]

Really? Although we might agree that worship *should* be all of those things, congregational worship often falls short of the ideal. Sometimes worship is joyful, sometimes depressingly somber; worship can acknowledge God's presence in the world, but it can also conceal it; believers may be transformed and renewed, or they may be bored; sometimes the faithful offer themselves to God's service in the world, sometimes they want to escape from unpleasant reality. Like all human responses to God, worship is ambiguous. So, while it is appropriate to talk about what worship should be, it is at least as important to be honest about what worship *is* in congregations of real people.

Praying and Believing

A funny thing has happened to our talk about worship. The word *worship* is a perfectly good verb and noun; it expresses both an action and an event. Recently, however, *worship* has become an adjective, as in "worship experience." This common usage is revealing, for it makes human experience the primary, substantive reality, with the modifier *worship* as only one among many forms of experience. The odd phrase *worship experience* reflects a shift away from glorifying God, toward what worship can do to fulfill us. It directs us away from God's gracious action in the world and toward our feelings. Because American culture encourages us to view life as a succession of experiences designed to bring us satisfaction, worship may become just one in an array of potentially fulfilling experiences. In a market-oriented consumer society, the "value" of worship is measured by its ability to satisfy.

The need to satisfy may lead to hymns, prayers, calls to worship, and sermons that are more about ourselves than the triune God who creates and sustains all things, who reconciles the world in Jesus Christ, who is at work among us as the Spirit of life. For instance, some of the hymns we sing in worship are hymns of praise to God:

> Sing praise to God, who reigns above,
> The God of all creation,
> The God of power, the God of love,
> The God of our salvation;
> With healing balm my soul is filled,
> And every faithless murmur stilled:
> To God all praise and glory![3]

Others focus on our response to God:

> O Lord my God! When I in awesome wonder
> Consider all the worlds Thy hands have made,
> I see the stars, I hear the rolling thunder,
> Thy power throughout the universe displayed;
> Then sings my soul, my Savior God, to Thee,
> How great Thou art . . .[4]

However, some invite us to sing about ourselves:

> We are one in the Spirit, We are one in the Lord . . .
> We will walk with each other, We will walk hand in hand . . .
> We will work with each other, we will work side by side . . .
> And they'll know we are Christians by our love . . .[5]

And:

> Called as partners in Christ's service, Called to ministries of grace,
> We respond with deep commitment Fresh new lines of faith to trace.
> May we learn the art of sharing, Side by side and friend with friend,
> Equal partners in our caring To fulfill God's chosen end.[6]

Apart from the question of whether we speak the truth when we sing about ourselves, people-centered worship is different from God-centered worship, both in intent and effect. One is celebration of ourselves; the other is an act of gratitude for God's love and grace, of hope in God's justice and mercy. Worship in the Reformed tradition centers on God rather than on our feelings and ourselves. "For what is the purpose of the preaching of the Word, of the sacraments, of religious gatherings, and of the whole external order of the church," asks Calvin, "except to unite us with God?"[7] Reformed worship is committed to worship in which God's initiative is primary. God calls us to worship, speaks to us, gives himself to us, and sends us to participate in the new Way inaugurated in Christ.

There is always a danger that Reformed worship's focus on God can become divorced from human realities, assuming an abstract, remote quality. Liturgical historian James White characterizes Reformed liturgy as "the most cerebral of the western traditions . . . prolix and verbose . . . overwhelmingly cerebral."[8] Reformed worshipers sometimes gaze longingly at neighboring churches, craving Episcopal grandeur, Methodist warmth, Baptist simplicity, or Pentecostal fervor. While worship in Reformed churches may be conducted "decently and in order," our Sunday mornings can be inundated by a torrent of words, drowning our genuine concerns. Reformed worship can be proper, but impersonal.

Lights and banners, dramas and dancers, dialogue sermons and multimedia presentations, cantatas and praise bands have all been tried in the attempt to make worship interesting and engaging. The most widespread strategy, evident in traditional and contemporary worship alike, is an unrelenting concentration on human potential, on worship designed to enlist religion as an ally in our quest for self-fulfillment. In too many congregations, worship is designed to help us "get something out of worship"—inspiration, peace of mind, a respite from the preceding week or a jump start for the coming week, guidance for living, support for family life, and more. Worship may also be designed to enhance institutional self-fulfillment, proliferating Sundays that promote congregational or denominational concerns. Too often, worship becomes a means to achieve personal or institutional ends rather than the praise of God from whom all blessings flow.

We are not faced with the false choice of worship that attends to God while neglecting human realities, or worship that concentrates on human needs and aspirations while slighting God. Because God reaches out in love to all creation and to every person, our worship of God opens us to the Source of all that is good. We are invited to worship the God who gives life in abundance. It makes a difference whether worship begins with people, providing God as one response to the need for human fulfillment, or with the God to whom people respond and thereby discover fulfillment. The Christian life—including Christian worship—promises love, joy, and peace. While human fulfillment may be a consequence of our worship, it is not the purpose of our worship of God. Christ came that we might have life, and have it abundantly (John 10:10), but faith's accent is on *Christ's* coming and the life *Christ* brings, not on abundant life that can be attained in many ways (including but not limited to Christ). Ironically, worship that concentrates on our needs and ourselves rather than on God ultimately fails to fulfill us. God is not a means to achieve human ends; only when our chief end is to glorify God will we enjoy God forever.[9]

Preserving worship's focus on God is more than a purist attempt to observe liturgical niceties. Christian faith itself is at stake, for the church's worship is a primary generator of the church's faith. An old Latin phrase, *lex orandi, lex credendi* (law of praying, law of believing) is a shorthand way of saying that the church's worship molds its belief (what is prayed shapes what is believed) as surely as the church's belief molds its worship (what is believed shapes what is prayed). Clearly, the hymns we sing (and those we avoid), the sacraments we celebrate (or neglect), what we pray for (and what we ignore in prayer), the vestments ministers wear (or shun), the ways we participate (or remain passive) influence the contours of belief within the congregation. Thus, the Reformed concern for worship that is theologically faithful grows from the recognition that the faith of the church is formed by the worship of the church.

Calvin's marks of a true church concern worship: "Wherever we see the Word of God purely preached and heard, and the sacraments administered according to Christ's institution, there, it is not to be doubted, a church of God exists."[10] Both marks concern the *practice* of worship, not simply how we *think* about worship, and both marks involve the *whole congregation,* not simply the *minister.* Calvin understood that the renewal of the church's faith and faithfulness begins with the renewal of worship in congregations. Reformed churches are blessed with marvelous resources for vital congregational worship: directories for worship, hymnals and psalters, contemporary songbooks, books of liturgies and prayers, journals, and magazines. For all their strengths, these resources alone cannot reform either the church's worship or its faith. Worship is not books; worship is the action of congregations. Only as ministers, sessions and consistories, musicians, and other worship leaders combine liturgical resources with faithful liturgical practice will worship exhibit truly the grace of the Lord Jesus Christ, the love of God, and the communion of the Holy Spirit.

Praise and thanks that unite us to God center on the Word of God. The Presbyterian Church's Directory for Worship declares that "Scripture—the Word written, preaching—the Word proclaimed, and the Sacraments—the Word enacted and sealed, bear testimony to Jesus Christ, the living Word."[11] When congregations gather for worship, Bible, pulpit, baptismal font, and communion table display the centrality of the Word written, preached, and enacted, bearing witness to the reality of the Word made flesh, the presence among us of God's grace and truth. We gather to worship at the invitation of the Word of God, not merely at the summons of desire or habit.

The Word Written

Congregational worship is the Bible's natural location. Before Scripture finds its way into the church school, committee meetings, personal devotions, private study, or scholarly examination, it lives in the congregation's worship. Detached from gratitude and praise of God, Scripture can become a mere textbook or instruction manual. While the Bible is marginal in many study groups and meetings, and no longer a staple of personal and family life, it may be that this "strange silence of the Bible in the church" is a direct result of its neglect in worship. The Bible is not absent from worship, of course; every Sunday service includes one or more Scripture readings. The simple act of reading passages from the Old and New Testaments does not mean that the Word written is permitted to bear testimony to Jesus Christ, the living Word. In an age when fewer people read and study the Scriptures regularly, many Christians become familiar with the Bible only as they hear it read aloud in Sunday morning worship.

Contemporary Christians who only hear the Bible are no different from most Christians throughout history, as well as Christians in many parts of the world today. Historically, believers have encountered the Word written, not by reading, but by hearing. Nevertheless, neglect of the Bible by too many North American Reformed Christians raises the question of how they might be helped to hear truly the Word written in worship.

An increasing number of congregations hear the Scriptures read according to the Revised Common Lectionary, an ecumenically ordered cycle of readings from the Old Testament, the New Testament letters, and the Gospels. Other congregations follow *lectio continua*, sequential Sunday readings, and preaching through a book of the Bible. Lectionaries provide congregations with disciplined exposure to the whole Bible, not simply to a minister's favorite passages. Yet lectionaries, by themselves, do not address the needs of worshipers whose exposure to the Bible is limited to hearing. Because so many people in the congregation are unfamiliar with the Scriptures, the reading of disjointed scriptural snippets does not allow the Bible to be clearly heard. Introducing a reading by intoning, "The Old Testament lesson is taken from the sixteenth chapter of Ezekiel, verses 59 through 63," does not provide adequate preparation for people who are unsure who Ezekiel was, when he spoke the word of the Lord, to whom he spoke, or the texture of his message, not to mention who doubt that ancient Ezekiel has anything to do with current realities.

The Directory for Worship is right when it says, "Listening to the reading of Scripture requires expectation and concentration,"[12] but both are difficult when worshipers have little idea what they are hearing. Congregations deserve adequate preparation for hearing so that the Word written may be given its voice. Preparing worshipers to hear Scripture readings should include a brief verbal introduction to the text and a prayer for the Spirit's aid in listening. Lengthy historical introductions are unnecessary, for they may serve only to distance the reading from its hearers. The primary aim is to help worshipers know what to listen for so that they can hear God's contemporary word to them. Perhaps then, believers will be encouraged to read as well as hear the scriptural message about God and God's Way in the world.

The Word Proclaimed

Preaching has always been at the center of Reformed worship. Sanctuaries usually feature large, prominent pulpits even if the communion table is shoved back against the wall and the baptismal font is concealed somewhere between the pulpit and the first row of pews. Congregations in search of a pastor invariably list good preaching as one of their highest priorities. What is good preaching? What happens when the congregational flow of praying, singing, reading, and moving about gives way to a time reserved for the pastor to speak?

In a culture dominated by television, the Internet, Facebook, and Twitter, there is something vaguely old-fashioned about a person standing before a group and talking for twenty minutes or so. It becomes startling when coupled with the assertion that the speaker is proclaiming the very word of God! Among God's many gifts to us, says Calvin, "it is a singular privilege that he deigns to consecrate to himself the mouths and tongues of men in order that his voice may resound in them."[13] The declaration that preaching *is* the word of God may seem audacious, but it is not a mere relic from a more credulous age. In our own time, Reformed theologians have continued to claim, "The Word of God preached now means . . . man's language about God in which and through which God Himself speaks about Himself."[14]

Haven't we all heard enough dreadful sermons to doubt that God's voice resounds in preachers' mouths? Haven't we heard enough questionable words from the pulpit to lose confidence that God speaks whenever pastors preach? Grand claims for preaching appear diminished when confronted with the reality of careless, uninformed, opinionated, compliant, or self-serving sermons. Yet the claims do not depend on the wisdom or skill of those who speak. Good preaching need not be eloquent or ingenious, amusing or erudite. Good preaching grows from fidelity to the scriptural witness, a refusal to conform to current cultural values. Good preaching is a human attempt to proclaim God's Way in Jesus Christ, inviting people to hear something new and to trust that the news is good. What is true of praying holds for preaching as well: Pastors do not know how to preach as they ought, yet they preach boldly, knowing that the Holy Spirit intercedes for them with sighs too deep for words (cf. Romans 8:26). How can we be confident that pastors are proclaiming God's Way and not the culture's way, or the church's way, or their own way?

The Directory for Worship mandates that "the preached Word or sermon is to be based upon the written Word. It is a proclamation of Scripture in the conviction that through the Holy Spirit Jesus Christ is present to the gathered people, offering grace and calling for obedience."[15] The directory is surely right in saying that preaching must be based upon the Bible, but it may be misleading when it calls the sermon a "proclamation of Scripture." Sermons should proclaim God's Way in Jesus Christ, ensuring the fidelity of proclamation by obedience to the scriptural witness. Pastors are not called to "preach the Bible," but to preach the gospel of God's Way in the world—the grace of the Lord Jesus Christ, the love of God, and the communion of the Holy Spirit—revealed through the witness of Scripture.

The difference between preaching the Bible and preaching the Way of God is more than hair-splitting. It is the difference between analyzing a pair of glasses and using the glasses to see more clearly, the difference between looking at a window and looking through it. Sermons that aim to tell people what the Bible says draw attention to the book itself, often creating distance between puzzling religious writings and a mystified congregation. Genuinely biblical preaching does not place pastors between Bible and congregation, presenting them as the designated interpreters who explain the book to people. In biblical preaching, pastors stand with the congregation, helping people look through the window at God's Way in the world; pastors sit with the congregation, looking through the spectacles that bring Christ into clear focus. It is the duty and task of preachers to bring people to the window, to fit them for glasses, not to tell people what the preacher alone can see.

As an aid to congregational vision, preaching is never the solitary act of the person in the pulpit. Remember that Calvin's first mark of the church is where the Word of God is rightly preached *and heard*. Congregations are not passive recipients of preacherly discourse, but partners with the preacher in listening for God's word, looking for God's Way. When pastor and congregation listen and look together, they will hear God's grace and see God's new creation. For Calvin, and for the mainstream of the Reformed tradition, hearing and seeing the Word are not only intellectual and imaginative. To *hear* the Word faithfully is to *do* the Word. The Reformed tradition joins with James in saying, "Be doers of the word, and not merely hearers who deceive themselves" (James 1:22).

The Word Enacted and Sealed

Reformed Christians are relatively comfortable talking about a church where the Word of God is purely preached and heard. Yet most Reformed churches neglect the sacraments, relegating the Sacrament of Baptism and the Lord's Supper to the fringes of worship. Reformed churches tend to be not churches of the Word and Sacrament, but churches of the Word alone. If Word and sacraments together are the heart of the church's true and faithful life, neglect of one leads inexorably to deformation of the other. When either Word or sacrament exists alone it soon becomes a parody of itself. Reformed Christians are aware of how easily the sacraments can become manipulative superstitions in churches where sacraments are exalted and preaching is minimized. We may be less aware of how easily preaching and teaching can deteriorate into institutional marketing, or human potential promotion, or bourgeois conformity in churches that magnify preaching while marginalizing the Sacrament of Baptism and Eucharist. Reformed neglect of the sacraments leads to a church of the Word alone, a church always in danger of degenerating into a church of mere words.

The need for a church of the Word *and sacrament* is not just a cure for terminal wordiness. It is not a matter of supplementing left-brain thinking with right-brain feeling, or replacing sharp words with warm communal affections, or suppressing the Word's judgment in favor of creating group ties that bind the church together. Word and sacrament are not contrasting aspects of church life: brain and heart, abstract and concrete. On the contrary, Calvin placed Word and sacrament *together* at the core of the church's life because he took it as "a settled principle that the sacraments have the same office as the Word of God: to offer and set forth Christ to us, and in him the treasures of heavenly grace."[16] Calvin's view is remarkable in two ways. First, the purpose of the sacraments is the same as that of the Word. Baptism and Eucharist have the same function as Scripture and preaching: to proclaim the truth of the gospel of Jesus Christ, giving us true knowledge of God. Second, the purpose of both is to communicate the presence of the living Christ to us, uniting us to him in the power of the Holy Spirit. The Word is not for imparting information and the sacraments are not for imparting feelings; both are occasions for the real presence of Christ in our midst.

Calvin was confident that Word and sacraments are effective: They give to us precisely what they portray. Preaching God's Word imparts Christ himself to us, maintaining Christ's living presence among us. The sacraments re-present the person and work of Christ, making real among us the presence of Christ. "I say that Christ is the matter or (if you prefer) the substance of all the sacraments," says Calvin, "for in him they have all their firmness, and they do not promise anything apart from him."[17] Thus, the Lord's Supper and the Sacrament of Baptism are not occasions for the Christian community merely to celebrate its own life. The sacraments impart to the community the substance of its life in Christ.

Word and sacrament together are instances of the real presence of Christ. In the Sacrament of Baptism and Eucharist, *Christ* is present to the community of faith. In a way that is not dependent on the ability or predilections of preachers and teachers, the sacraments proclaim the gospel, depicting the good news in bold relief. Thus, Reformed neglect of the sacraments has muted the gospel's proclamation, both by an absence of Christ's sacramental presence and by a sacramental gap in union with Christ. Hearing and seeing is not the end of the matter. God's grace can also be touched, tasted, and smelled. As people share the waters of Baptism and the bread and wine of the Lord's Supper, they receive the grace of the Lord Jesus Christ, the love of God, and the communion of the Holy Spirit. The sacraments are the Word of God; they are not a different word from the witness of Scripture, nor do they diverge from the testimony of faithful preaching.

Baptism

In typical baptism services, everything focuses on celebrating the incorporation of a person, most often an infant, into the life of the congregation. The baptismal liturgy may include words of Scripture and prayers that describe a broader, deeper reality, but the action itself tends to narrow the sacrament to only one aspect of its significance. The folksy demeanor of the pastor, introductions of the family and friends, abbreviated readings and prayers, the minimal sight and sound of water, reminders of church programs, and the leisurely stroll through the congregation all combine to collapse meaning into the reception of a singular child into a particular congregation.

Baptism is the sacrament of welcome into the community of believers, of course, but it is not only that. Baptism's capacity to unite us to God in Christ through the power of the Holy Spirit is only hinted at in most baptismal services. A mere sample of New Testament baptismal texts reveals rich baptismal images cascading over one another in a stream of living water that resounds with

- discipleship (Matthew 28:16-20);
- forgiveness of sins and the gift of the Holy Spirit (Acts 2:37-42);

- response to the good news and life in the community of faith (Acts 10:44-48);
- dying and rising with Christ and union with Christ (Romans 6:1-11);
- a new exodus from slavery to freedom in Christ (1 Corinthians 10:1-4);
- union with sisters and brothers in Christ (1 Corinthians 12:12-13);
- distinctions no longer divisions (Galatians 3:26-29);
- new circumcision (Colossians 2:11-15);
- new covenant, new community, new openness to the world (1 Peter 3:18-22).

In short, baptism is a sign of the fullness of God's gracious love and effectual calling that, in one moment, is poured over a single human being. The moment is not isolated, a point in time that recedes into distant memory. Baptism is the sure promise of God's continuing faithfulness, inaugurating new life within God's Way. Baptism is far more than an unremembered event from our infancy, for every baptism is an act of the whole community of all the baptized. As we hear again gracious words of promise, confess the faith of the church in the words of the Apostles' Creed, join in the prayer of thanksgiving over the water, and speak words of welcome, we remember and affirm our own baptism. Baptism is the foundational event and continuing basis for our life in Christ. The 1559 Confession of the French Reformed Church puts it nicely: "In Baptism we are grafted into the body of Christ, washed and cleansed by his blood, and renewed in holiness of life by his Spirit. Although we are baptized only once, the benefit it signifies lasts through life and death, so that we have an enduring testimony that Jesus Christ will be our justification and sanctification forever."[18]

It is too small a thing that this ocean of meaning, deep and moving, should be reduced to a chummy ritual of congregational welcome. Limiting baptism deprives the congregation of an opportunity to remember the promises of God, to rejoice in God's redemption, and to renew the gift of life in Christ. Baptism does even more than present the fullness of the gospel. Baptism is a means of grace, *communicating and bringing about* the thing it signifies! Baptism does not merely tell us about Christ, or point to Christ, or signify Christ. In baptism, Christ is present with us as we are made one with him in a death like his so that we will become one with him in a resurrection like his. Baptism welcomes persons into the church by incorporation into the body of Christ, the one holy catholic apostolic church.

The task facing Reformed churches goes beyond the search for a proper understanding of baptism. The task is a reformation of baptismal practice. Following Calvin's lead, our task is to recover more faithful ways of administering and celebrating baptism so that the Word of God will be enacted within the congregation's worship. One mark of a faithful church is its faithful *doing* of baptism, its *performing* of God's Word so that all may behold God's goodness.

If baptism proclaims the gracious love of God, inviting a life of grateful response, why do Reformed churches baptize infants? Why not defer baptism until a person is old enough to understand God's grace, to respond in trust, and to request that the Word of God be sealed in baptism? In the Reformed tradition, baptism is understood as the preeminent sign of God's grace. Before a baby has a chance to be faithful or faithless, good or bad, the sure promise of God's love is present. Even when an adult believer is baptized, baptism is an instance of God's grace, not a response to human faith. Baptism always enacts God's Word, not our words.

The Lord's Supper
"It would be well," wrote Calvin, "to require that the Communion of the Holy Supper of Jesus Christ be held every Sunday at least as a rule."[19] Worshipers may shudder at the prospect. Many congregations celebrate "the joyful feast of the people of God" by sitting passively while the organ drones dolefully in the background, waiting for tiny cubes of bread and thimbles of grape juice to arrive. Others have adopted the more active practice of walking forward and communing by intinction, but the procession is likely to be silent and oddly private. Some congregations attempt to add spice to the Supper by changing it into an occasion of cheerful congregational camaraderie. Neither lonely introspection nor forced togetherness seems worth the effort it would take to hold "the Communion of the Holy Supper of Jesus Christ" every Sunday.

Calvin failed in his efforts to convince churches to celebrate the Lord's Supper every Lord's Day, although this was the practice of the early church and remains the practice of many churches today. For centuries, quarterly communion was typical Reformed practice, although recent years have brought more frequent celebrations of the sacrament. The Lord's Supper may be on the path to becoming a monthly rite, but an arbitrary designation of the first Sunday of the month as "communion Sunday" indicates its institutional rather than ecclesial function. Reformed reluctance to come to the Lord's Table weekly is the result both of diminished understanding of the Lord's Supper and of impoverished sacramental practice.

Even when we use the terms *communion* or *Eucharist* (from the Greek word for "thanksgiving") instead of *Lord's Supper*, the Church's celebration of the sacrament is invariably associated with the Last Supper. In an upper room on the night of his betrayal and arrest, Jesus took bread, and after giving thanks he broke it and gave it to his friends, saying, "Take, eat; this is my body which is given for you. Do this in remembrance of me." After supper, he did the same with wine, saying, "This cup is the new covenant in my blood. Do this in remembrance of me" (1 Corinthians 11:23–26; Mark 14:22–25; Matthew 26:26–29; Luke 22:14–23). We are right to remember that meal when we share bread and wine, but we are wrong to limit our remembrance to that one time and place.

In the first centuries of the church, the community gathered every Lord's Day, sometimes at risk to liberty or life, to share eucharistic bread and wine. The church did not gather every Thursday night, but every Sunday morning; the church did not come together in remembrance of the Last Supper, but in celebration of new life with the resurrected, living Lord. In the Gospels, eucharistic meals are dramatic features of Jesus' resurrection appearances. The risen, living Lord eats and drinks with his disciples. Perhaps the most familiar of these resurrection meals took place on the road to Emmaus: "When [the risen Christ] was at the table with them, he took bread, blessed and broke it, and gave it to them. Then their eyes were opened, and they recognized him" (Luke 24:30–31). The early church looked to resurrection meal texts more than to Last Supper texts because it recognized its own experience there. The community still ate and drank with the risen Christ, and in his presence they came to know him more fully and love him more deeply.

The church knew that eating and drinking with the Lord continued a pattern from Jesus' life. The narratives of the miraculous feeding of the thousands are explicitly eucharistic (Mark 6:30–44 and parallels). The church also remembered that Jesus was notorious for eating and drinking with sinners, and so the community knew that Jesus eats and drinks with sinners still. In all of this, the church hoped as well as remembered, looking to the great heavenly banquet when all the faithful would feast with God. No wonder the early church celebrated the Lord's Supper every Lord's Day! They were not commemorating the tragic death of a hero or mourning the premature death of an inspiring teacher. They were gathering in the presence of the risen, living Christ to be joined to him in his death and resurrection and to be fed by him, receiving nourishment for growth in the love of God and neighbors. If congregations experience the Lord's Supper only as a remembrance of Jesus' death, a recreation of the Last Supper, it is little wonder that they do it infrequently and that when they do they are vaguely puzzled or dissatisfied by it all.

Memory alone is not enough to sustain significant corporate life. For citizens of the United States, July 4 is Independence Day, the remembrance and celebration of the 1776 signing of the Declaration of Independence in Philadelphia. Although everyone knows the reason for the holiday, it no longer marks our participation in the deep national and personal significance of American independence as we reflect on the foundation of our liberties. The Fourth of July has become a mere midsummer holiday. We may go to a fireworks display, or even take in a parade, but none of it binds us to our liberties in a deeply communal celebration of our national independence. In the same way, celebrations of the birthdays of George Washington and Abraham Lincoln have been collapsed into an increasingly obscure Presidents Day, while Martin Luther King's birthday is fast becoming one more three-day weekend. Remembrance alone is not sufficient to sustain significance, so we reduce the number of times we try to force memory to do something new—thus, infrequent communion.

Reduction of Eucharist to an infrequent memorial of Jesus' death is also a factor in the un-Reformed reduction of church to a voluntary assemblage of individual believers. Calvin notes three benefits of the Lord's Supper: first, we receive Christ and participate in the blessings of his death and resurrection; second, we are led to recognize the continuing blessings of Christ and respond with lives of gratitude and praise; and third, we are roused to holy living, for by receiving Christ our lives are conformed to Christ. Calvin goes on to note that while conformity to Christ should be the reality in all parts of our life,

> yet it has a special application to charity, which is above all recommended to us in this sacrament; for which reason it [the Lord's Supper] is called the bond of charity. For as the bread, which is there sanctified for the common use of us all, is made of many grains so mixed together that one cannot be discerned from the other, so ought we to be united among ourselves in one indissoluble friendship. What is more: we all receive there the same body of Christ, in order that we may be made members of it.[20]

If the Lord is really present in his Supper, binding believers to himself and to one another, the absence of Eucharist may help to explain the fractured isolation that characterizes too many congregations and is a virtual description of denominational life. The risen Lord gives us himself in the bread and wine of communion, and yet we say "no, thank you" more Sundays than not. Merely increasing the frequency of communion will be unsatisfactory if eucharistic practice continues to promote silent introspection that distances believers from each other, the world, and even their Lord.

Reformed churches possess sufficient theological and liturgical resources to appreciate the substance of sacramental communion with the crucified and risen Christ. The theology that is expressed in liturgical texts envisions individual hearers of an individually preached Word becoming, in the Lord's Supper, a community bound in the grace of the Lord Jesus Christ, the love of God, and the communion of the Holy Spirit. Yet biblically faithful eucharistic theology and theologically faithful eucharistic texts are necessary, if not insufficient. If the Lord's Supper is to nourish one holy catholic and apostolic community, communion must be embodied in frequent eucharistic practice that enacts the fullness of the church's eucharistic theology and animates the church's rich eucharistic texts.

> Therefore, the sacraments have effectiveness among us in proportion as we are helped by their ministry sometimes to foster, confirm, and increase the

true knowledge of Christ in ourselves; at other times to possess him more fully and enjoy his riches. But that happens when we receive in true faith what is offered there.[21]

Form and Freedom in Worship

Worship in the Reformed tradition is ordered around the Word of God written, preached, and enacted as witness to the Word of God, Jesus Christ. Reformed churches have tended to distrust elaborations, ceremonies, and innovations, fearing that they will detract from the congregation's proper attention to the Word. While Reformed restraint in worship sometimes leads to worship that is barren and unresponsive to people of faith, restraint can be liberating, freeing congregations from frantic attempts to cater to conflicting desires. Preaching and sacraments, prayers and hymns, furnishings and robes, observances and anthems: all are subject to the Word of God, and all are useful only as they unite us with God.

Calvin provides us with a useful guideline as we shape congregational worship. Asked if his critique of medieval Catholic excesses in ceremonial worship means that no ceremonies are appropriate, he responds, "I do not say that. For I feel that this kind of help is very useful to them. I only contend that the means used ought to show Christ, not to hide him."[22]

1. Annie Dillard, *An American Childhood* (New York: Quality Paperback Book Club, 1990), p. 193.
2. Directory for Worship, W-1.1001.
3. "Sing Praise to God, Who Reigns Above," *The Presbyterian Hymnal* (Louisville: Westminster/John Knox Press, 1990), no. 483.
4. "How Great Thou Art," *The Presbyterian Hymnal*, no. 467.
5. "We Are One in the Spirit," *The Worshipbook* (Philadelphia: Westminster Press, 1970, 1972), Hymn 619.
6. "Called as Partners in Christ's Service," *The Presbyterian Hymnal*, no. 343.
7. Calvin, commentary on Psalm 24, in *Calvin: Commentaries*, ed. Joseph Haroutunian (Philadelphia: Westminster Press, 1958), p. 393.
8. James F. White, *Protestant Worship* (Louisville: Westminster/John Knox Press, 1989), pp. 58–78.
9. Shorter Catechism, *Book of Confessions*, 7.001.
10. Calvin, *Institutes*, 4.1.9.
11. Directory for Worship, W-1.1004.
12. Ibid., W-2.2006.
13. *Institutes*, 4.1.5.
14. Barth, *Church Dogmatics*, 1.1., p. 106.
15. Directory for Worship, W-2.2007.
16. *Institutes*, 4.14.17.
17. Ibid., 4.14.16.
18. *The French Confession of 1559*, XXXV, p. 16.
19. Calvin, "Articles concerning the Organization of the Church and of Worship at Geneva," in *Calvin: Theological Treatises*, ed. J. K. S. Reid (Philadelphia: Westminster Press, 1954), p. 49.
20. Calvin, "Short Treatise on the Holy Supper of our Lord," in *Calvin: Theological Treatises*, p. 151.
21. *Institutes*, 4.14.16.
22. Ibid., 4.19.14.

Community in an Age of Individualism

9

In general the churches, visited by me too often on weekdays—when the custodian was moving the communion table about like a packing case, and sweeping up the chewing-gum wrappers that insolently spangled the sacrosanct reaches of the choir—bore for me the same relation to God that billboards did to Coca-Cola: they promoted thirst without quenching it.

John Updike, A Month of Sundays[1]

We use the word *church* in a bewildering variety of ways. The church is buildings, people, congregations, organizations, denominations, and more. For the most part, we manage well enough with our multiple definitions for *church*. At least we think we do.

Imagine a group of fifth-graders in a church school class. If they are asked to do a free-association exercise, what will pop into their heads when they hear the word *church*?

> First Reformed Church . . . people who follow Jesus . . . singing hymns . . . boring . . . giving money . . . praying . . . Sunday . . . God . . . minister . . . *and so on and so on.*

We seldom ask fifth-graders to free associate, but they do it anyway whenever they hear "church," and so do we. Fifth-graders and fifty-year-olds carry in their heads a bundle of images associated with church. The images are unstable, shifting between personal involvement in the images and distance from them. There are times when we see ourselves as part of the picture: "People are singing hymns, and I am one of those people." At other times, we may be outside the picture: "The church is always asking me for money." (Alternatively, "*They* are always making us sing unsingable hymns"; or, "*We* are developing a fuller appreciation of stewardship.")

Because our jumbled images for church emerge from our experience, they are altered as our experiences change. The fifth-grader who thinks *boring* when he has to sit through the annual meeting of the congregation may think *people who follow Jesus* when his class visits a nursing home. Similarly, a person may think *the church is always asking for money* until she becomes a member of the stewardship committee;

115

then she may think of herself as part of "the church" that must encourage *a fuller appreciation of stewardship* in "them."

Visible and Invisible Church?

Christian thinking about the church is like looking through a kaleidoscope, with every move creating a different pattern. This leads to confusion in Christian talking about the church, for we can never be sure that people are referring to the same thing. Does "church" mean *us* or *them? near* or *far? institution* or *movement? holy* or *hypocritical? denomination* or *congregation* or *the church universal? friend* or *stranger?* The formal term for Christian thinking about the church is "ecclesiology," but ecclesiology can be as imprecise among theologians as among fifth-graders.

A fundamental source of confusion is the way we mix talk about the actual church and an ideal church. When we call the church "a chosen race, a royal priesthood, a holy nation, God's own people," are we saying something about real congregations in Pittsburgh, Paris, and Pretoria? . . . or are we speaking about a heavenly body? . . . or are we spinning a dream-wish? What, really, do we mean when we sing the second verse of the well-known hymn "The Church's One Foundation"?

> Elect from every nation, Yet one o'er all the earth,
> Her charter of salvation One Lord, one faith, one birth;
> One holy name she blesses, Partakes one holy food,
> And to one hope she presses, With every grace endued.[2]

The opening line claims a Christian unity that is not present in our own towns, let alone "o'er all the earth." We Christians claim that our fragmentation is enveloped by a spiritual unity, but we are unable to point to many signs of our oneness in the Spirit. Agreement in "one faith" is lacking within denominations, let alone among them. While we may bless one holy name, partaking one holy food is often prohibited in each other's churches. We stagger toward conflicting hopes, and do a good job of concealing our endued graces. "The Church's One Foundation" is a wonderful hymn, but the church it sings about seems to be an ideal, not the experienced reality of women and men struggling to carry the tune. Yet, as we sing the hymn time after time, we come to know "church" as a theological concept that differs from the experienced reality of everyday life. The discrepancy between concept and reality is puzzling at best.

Many Christians try to clear up the confusion by differentiating the church we sing about from the churches in which we sing. The distinction is phrased in a number of ways: ideal/real, invisible/visible, inner/outer, pure/worldly, essential/empirical, true/actual. Common to all is the notion that the church has a dual nature that can be reconciled by conceiving of the ideal church as a model to which the actual church should conform. Since the actual church embodies beliefs and practices that do not measure up to the pure faith and life of the ideal church, the actual church "ought to be" what the ideal church "is." Although this method of harmonizing confused language about the church is common among members and scholars alike, it turns real and ideal upside down: the ideal church becomes the *real* thing, while the actual church is reduced to a pale imitation.

People are drawn to the church for an assortment of reasons, bringing a mixture of faith and doubt, commitment and apathy. What we find in the church is a similar mixture of faithfulness and hypocrisy, care and indifference, bold witness and crass conformity, ministry and self-serving. In an attempt to ward off disillusionment, we are told (and tell ourselves?) that what we experience is not the true church; the *true* church is purer, holier, and more faithful than what we see around us. To the extent that we believe such talk, it only promotes frustration and guilt: frustration that we experience something far less glorious than it is supposed to be, guilt that the church constantly fails to be what it "is."

How long can we hear talk about the distinction between the "true reality" of the ideal church and the "deficient reality" of the actual church before we begin to hold the actual church in contempt? Notions of "ideal church" lead inevitably to disparagement of the actual church that never measures up. This causes some people to abandon an actual congregation (or denomination) for one that promises to be purer. Others leave the church altogether, perhaps in anger, but more often in disillusionment. Yet even those of us who remain are not immune to the harm done by the distinction between the ideal and actual church. How do we continue to be part of a community that claims to be the body of Christ but is so obviously flawed by lovelessness, error, injustice, and sin? How do we maintain trust in an organization that proclaims itself to be holy yet is so often indistinguishable (except negatively) from social service agencies, volunteer fire departments, or the Kiwanis? We often manage by claiming that within the drab husk of the church we experience lays a pure kernel of truth and constancy. What we see is not all we get. This conviction may lead some to work for the church's reform, but, just as often, it leads to mere institutional loyalties that excuse routine faithlessness and live with habitual evils.

Reformed Reality

Reformed thinking about the church has always been marked by utter realism. Beginning with Calvin, Reformed theology has avoided ideal images of the church, looking instead at the real life of congregations called to faithfulness by God. Although Calvin distinguishes between the *invisible church* (true children of God by grace) and the *visible church* (everyone who professes Christ, whether truly or not), his is no more than a commonsense observation: Some within the church do not live God's grace, and only God knows who are his own. The distinction between visible and invisible has scant relevance to Calvin's thinking about the church. Since only God can see the invisible church, Calvin focuses on the only church *we* can see, a visibly human mixture of faith and faithlessness. "A Reformed narrative of the church has no Eden," says Amy Plantinga Pauw. "The church on earth has always existed 'after the fall.' "[3] What we see is what we get . . . *all* we get.

The visible church—all of the obviously flawed congregations and denominations we see around us—*is* the church, the only church there is. The visible church is the true church, not because it conforms to an ideal model, but because it is the community of men and women called by God, redeemed by Jesus Christ, and empowered by the Holy Spirit. A church is not a church by virtue of its own efforts or achievements, but only by the grace of God who calls women and men to share new life in Christ through the power of the Holy Spirit. Dutch theologian G. C. Berkouwer expresses the Reformed view: "The *credo ecclesiam* does not direct our attention only to what ought to be and what ought to happen, but to what obviously has happened in the lives of those who, according to the words of the Belgic Confession, 'bow their necks under the yoke of Jesus Christ' (Art. 28)."[4]

The church is not always a pretty sight. As often as not we gaze upon collections of ordinary people whose personal and ecclesial lives are marred by all-too-visible failings. Must we be content with all that we see in the church, overlooking everything from personal pettiness to corporate evil? Of course not. The church is not exempt from scrutiny; we can and must assess the church's faith and life at all times. Our critique should not evaluate the actual church against an ideal image, but against the gospel of Christ's grace, God's love, and the communion of the Holy Spirit. As we have seen, Calvin measures church life against two benchmarks: Is the actual church a place where the Word of God is rightly preached and heard, and is it a place where the sacraments are celebrated in fidelity to Christ? Calvin's standard is not a static abstraction. Instead, he calls for dynamic auditing of the church's proclamation: Does the church preach, teach, celebrate, and live the good news of God's grace in Jesus Christ? The gospel, not a figment of our imagination, is the sole criterion for judging the church.

Proclamation of the gospel is never faultless in any church, of course. Could we find a congregation or denomination where the Word of God is *purely* preached and heard? Is there a church where the sacraments are *truly* administered according to Christ's institution? No. Every church's fidelity to the gospel is flawed by flimsy proclamation, diluted sacraments, and an all-too-apparent shortage of ears that hear. Yet, says Calvin, although we can see that every church "swarms with many faults," we are not to become people "who, imbued with a false conviction of their own perfect sanctity . . . spurn association with all men in whom they discern any remnant of human nature."[5] We will never find a church that is free from fault, nor will our own judgments ever be immune to self-serving error.

North American culture encourages individual judgment, distrusting the conformist impulses of groups and the coercive power of institutions. The individual person is thought to be the final arbiter of truth, the sole judge of what is right and wrong. Thus, churches are treated like other voluntary organizations in society: We grant them approval and a measure of participation as long as they reflect our views. If they speak and act in ways that conflict with our convictions, we feel free to withhold our support or withdraw our participation. North American confidence in the priority of the individual works a not-too-subtle change in churches themselves. If congregations are seen as voluntary organizations, then they feel constrained to act that way, appealing to personal preferences to gain allegiance. "Meeting people's needs" can easily become churchly code for "giving people what they want." Since what people want is not always identical to God's Way, churches may unwittingly substitute the standard of program appeal for the criterion of the gospel, ordering congregational life by its capacity to attract members rather than by fidelity to Christ.

Calvin was fully aware of the church's ever-possible and ever-present error in both faith and life. Nevertheless, he believed that the church has first claim on us, not the other way around. The church, says Calvin, is our mother in the faith:

> There is no way to enter into life unless this mother conceive us in her womb, give us birth, nourish us at her breast, and lastly, unless she keep us under her care and guidance. . . . Our weakness does not allow us to be dismissed from her school until we have been pupils all our lives.[6]

It is through the proclamation of the community of faith that we come to new life in Christ, through the proclamation of the congregation that we are schooled in the faith, through the proclamation of the church that we are guided in God's Way. No church is perfect, just as no mother is perfect, yet both have claims on us that transcend our choosing.

Calvin's high regard for a church replete with obvious faults is not a quaint sixteenth-century sentiment, but an enduring feature of Reformed ecclesiology. In our own time, Karl Barth vigorously criticized the church's failings, yet confessed,

> I believe that the congregation to which I belong, in which I have been called to faith and am responsible for my faith, in which I have my service, is the one holy, universal Church. If I do not believe this here, I do not believe it at all. No lack of beauty, no "wrinkles and spots" in this congregation

may lead me astray. . . . There is no sense, when seeking after the "true" congregation, in abandoning one's concrete congregation.[7]

What causes seemingly sensible people to place such faith in a human community they know "swarms with many faults"? Have Calvin, Barth, and other Reformed theologians fallen prey to the self-interest of the ecclesiastically privileged? Is their confidence in the flawed human community called "church" grounded in the good news of God's continuing presence?

The Body of Christ, the Community of the Holy Spirit

The church—denomination or congregation—is a thoroughly human community of thoroughly human men and women. It is neither infallible nor perfect. It is often faithless and sometimes dangerous. Once we have catalogued every dismal failing, we can go on to affirm that the church is the body of Christ, the community of the Holy Spirit, a group of being-saved people in whom and through whom God is always present. At the conclusion of worship, pastors often pronounce the apostolic benediction: "The grace of the Lord Jesus Christ, the love of God, and the communion of the Holy Spirit, be with you all." This *communion* of the Holy Spirit is the *community of*, the *participation in* the Holy Spirit. Celebrating the Spirit's descent at Pentecost is more than a silly celebration of "the church's birthday"; it is our recognition of the inauguration of God's continuing presence with God's people, the ongoing formation of one holy catholic and apostolic church.

The New Testament contains many images for the church. Prominent among them is the church as the body of Christ. The body of Christ texts—1 Corinthians 12, Romans 12, Ephesians 1 and 4, and Colossians 1—provide us with surprising insight into the life of the contemporary church. Each text, in language known to most Christians, probes implications of the church as the body of Christ. Our familiarity with the New Testament's body of Christ passages may diminish their capacity to help us understand the church. We have heard them so often, in classes and sermons and even church publicity, that we think we have heard it all. "Body of Christ," the Bible's shocking metaphor, has become a cliché.

"Human organizations are like the human body" is a modern truism. The comparison is embedded in everyday references to "the body politic," "a body of troops," and "legislative bodies," not to mention less obvious allusions to "corporate life." The Presbyterian Church (U.S.A.) even calls its sessions, presbyteries, synods, and the General Assembly "governing bodies." Unfortunately, such conventional uses of the organization-body figure of speech shape the way New Testament body of Christ texts are understood in the church. Each of us has something to contribute to the whole church (so the story goes) and the church is incomplete without the diverse gifts of its members. The church cannot be whole without all of its members, and none of its members can go it alone. Whether in its congregational form (singers, organizers, educators, kitchen workers, and caregivers are all needed to make the church's life whole) or in its denominational form (liberals, conservatives, evangelists, social activists, bureaucrats, and pastors need each other to be complete), the comparison of the church to the body is a commonplace. The church-body analogy has scant capacity to inform us, let alone to alter the way we live.

Correlation between an organization and the human body is not only a modern platitude; it was already a cliché in the first century. The human organization as body was a well-known Hellenistic figure of speech, used to describe the *polis* and the family as well as other institutions and associations.[8] Comparing any organization to the human body was little more than first-century conventional wisdom. If Paul had been doing nothing more than noting that diverse persons in the church need each other to function together as a unified whole, the readers of his letters might have dismissed his body language as a truism. Paul was not being trite. He had something to say that was—and is—surprising.

When we look closely at the body of Christ passages in the New Testament we quickly move beyond conventional understandings. The texts do far more than compare the human organization, the church, to the one-yet-differentiated human organism, the body. Neither 1 Corinthians nor Romans nor Ephesians nor Colossians says simply that the church is *like* the human body. Instead, they make the startling claim that the church *is* the body *of Christ.*

As if this were not enough—*we* are the body *of Christ, we* are one body *in Christ, we* are the body whose *head is Christ*—the texts suggest that we are Christ's *wounded* body, even Christ's *crucified* body. The suffering, executed, dead, and buried Jesus has been raised to new life, of course, but resurrection does not eradicate crucifixion. The crucified one is raised, and the resurrected one is none other than the crucified. As the body *of Christ,* the church is not a glorified body. The church is the body of the crucified-risen Christ, and so the church lives with nail marks in its hands and a gash in its side (John 20:24–29), as a slaughtered lamb (Revelation 5), and as the body whose hands and feet remain pierced (Luke 24:36–49).

The church does not live in triumphant glory, although there are times when the church pretends to itself and others that it is a powerful force in the world. The pretense is difficult to maintain in the current era of the church's cultural marginalization, even though nostalgia and wishful thinking are present. The New Testament's body of Christ texts draw us back to the cross as they proclaim the Lord's death until he comes (1 Corinthians 11:26). The church is made Christ's body through baptism into Christ's death: "For in the one Spirit we were all baptized into one body" (1 Corinthians 12:13). Christ continues to offer bread, nourishing the church-body: "Take; this is my body" (Mark 14:22). The church has been united with Christ in a death like his, and the fullness of resurrection is not yet its possession (Romans 6:5). Thus, the church's bodily existence as the church of the cross is not an unfortunate necessity, but the God-given shape of its life as the body of Christ.

The church is the wounded body of Christ. Paul's body of Christ passages in letters to Corinth, Rome, Ephesus, and Colossae neither celebrate the church's diversity nor applaud its unity. He employs the metaphor in contexts of discord and division, not peace and harmony. "Is Christ divided?" Paul asks the Corinthians. His question is more than rhetorical and the answer remains uncertain. From first-century Corinth through Christian communities spanning twenty centuries, the grotesque reality is that the disciples of Christ lacerate and tear the suffering body of Christ.

"Body of Christ" is used throughout Paul's letters at points of conflict and division in the church. The book of 1 Corinthians is laced with recognition of dissensions, quarreling, factionalism, and strife. The conflict within the community demonstrates dramatically that members of the body of Christ have a common need for diverse gifts. Recognition of this reality leads to "care for one another" in the "more excellent way" that "does not insist on its own way." The split between Jewish Christians and Gentile Christians in Rome leads Paul to use "body of Christ" again, bracketed by admonitions that no one should "think of himself more highly than he ought to think" and exhortations to "love one another with brotherly affection" and to "live peaceably with all." Even the loftier letter to the Ephesians acknowledges the continuing division of Jews and Gentiles, coupling "one body" with the plea to live "forbearing one another in love . . . maintaining the unity of the Spirit in the bond of peace." In Colossians the link between Christ's suffering and the church's suffering is explicit: "I am now rejoicing in my sufferings for your sake, and in my flesh I am completing what is lacking in Christ's afflictions for the sake of his body, that is, the church" (Colossians 1:24).

Therefore, to call the church "body of Christ" is more than acknowledging that the human community of Christ's people is like the human body. The church is not merely a human community with the brand name "Christian." Because Christ is present in this body, the body is no longer its own, but Christ's. Because the risen Christ still bears the wounds, the church is not triumphant, but the wounded body of Christ. In Amy Plantinga Pauw's lovely phrase, the church is a community of "graced infirmity."

Talk about the church as a marvelous collection of diverse human talents is not wrong, but neither does it express what Paul means by "the body of Christ." As Christ's body, the church is composed of persons to whom God has given spiritual gifts necessary for their common life in Christ. The church, like any body, may need an array of talents: sopranos, accountants, cooks, managers, artists, babysitters, and carpenters. Church members possessing some of these needed talents can and should give their talents as gifts to the community. Spiritual gifts are a different matter. Paul does not write about our natural talents and abilities, but about new capacities for new life in a new community of faith. God graces the community with what it needs to be the body *of Christ* in the world. An individual congregation may not have all the talent it needs to be a successful organization; it does have the spiritual gifts it needs to be the body of Christ.

"Now there are varieties of gifts," says Paul, "but the same Spirit. . . . To each is given the manifestation of the Spirit for the common good" (1 Corinthians 12:4, 7). The Holy Spirit gifts each person within the church, and this diversity of spiritual gifts comprises the whole body of Christ. Spiritual gifts include wisdom and knowledge, prophecy and discernment, teaching and exhorting, healing and tongues, leadership and generosity, and many more. Paul's lists of gifts are not exhaustive catalogs, but illustrations of the ways God equips the community for new life. Love is the identifying mark of every spiritual gift, and all gifts are given for the common good of the whole community. No one person receives all of the Spirit's gifts. Instead, within each community of faith different people receive different gifts, providing the church with everything it needs for faithful ministry and mission. God does not abandon the church to muddle through on its own power. God is present and active among God's people, graciously providing what the community needs.

Gifts of the Spirit are not reserved for a limited number of special people within the church, unavailable to the masses. "To *each* is given the manifestation of the Spirit *for the common good*" (1 Corinthians 12:7). The Spirit gifts each person in the church; every person's gifts contribute to the wholeness of the body *of Christ.* The gifts of God are not treasured possessions, reserved for private pleasure; we are to use God's gifts to us for building up the body *of Christ.* Precisely because the gifts of the Spirit build up the body *of Christ,* they are not the church's precious property, available for its exclusive benefit; we are to use the gifts in service to others. As the body *of Christ,* the church is given its character by the one who came not to be served, but to serve (Mark 10:45). Paul is clear about the connection between the gifts of the Spirit and the service of Christ: "Now there are varieties of gifts, but the same Spirit; and there are varieties of services, but the same Lord" (1 Corinthians 12:4, 5). God's gifts are to be used to build up the body of Christ for service in the world.

Because it is the body *of Christ,* the church is called to forms of service that derive their character from the Lord. The Confession of 1967 acknowledges that "The life, death, resurrection, and promised coming of Jesus Christ has set the pattern for the church's mission. . . . The church follows this pattern in the form of its life and in the method of its action. So to live and serve is to confess Christ as Lord."[9] The church does not always follow this pattern, of course. The church may refuse the Spirit's gifts and avoid Christ's service, preferring to rely on its own assets and serve its own needs. Yet even then, God does not abandon the community. Christ remains present among us "to seek and to save the lost," and the Holy Spirit continues with us "to guide you into all the truth."

Organization

"Each of us was given grace according to the measure of Christ's gift," says Paul. "The gifts he gave were that some would be apostles, some prophets, some evangelists, some pastors and teachers, to equip the saints for the work of ministry, for building up the body of Christ" (Ephesians 4:7, 11-12). From the earliest days of the church, it has been recognized that some form of organization is useful in ordering the ministry of the whole people of God. While the New Testament displays diverse, fluid patterns of organization, the church soon developed the threefold model of bishop, priest, and deacon. Calvin's reading of the New Testament and his assessment of "the present condition of the Church" led him to institute a fourfold model:

- pastor, responsible for preaching the Word and administering the sacraments;
- doctor or teacher, responsible for scriptural interpretation and the purity of doctrine;
- elder, responsible for discipline and oversight; and
- deacon, charged with administering alms and caring for the sick and needy.

Calvin knew that forms of church organization are not divinely ordained. Although he believed that the Scriptures express everything necessary to salvation, he also believed that the Lord "did not will in outward discipline and ceremonies to prescribe in detail what we ought to do (because he foresaw that this depended upon the state of the times, and he did not deem one form suitable for all ages)." Thus, he concluded, the organization of the church, always in the service of the building of the church, "ought to be variously accommodated to the customs of each nation and age."[10] Calvin's form of church organization for sixteenth-century Geneva was "variously accommodated" as Reformed churches were established throughout Europe and carried to America.

Most Reformed churches maintain a threefold pattern of ordered ministry within the ministry of the whole people of God: ministers of the Word and Sacrament, elders, and deacons. Ordered ministry does not distinguish clergy from laity: All people in the church are laity (from the Greek *laos theou*, "people of God"), and two of the church's three ordered offices are filled by persons commonly called "laypeople." Ministry of the Word and Sacrament is but one of the three ordered ministries in the church, and all three are exercises of leadership on behalf of the whole church.

On behalf of the *whole* church. Within the Reformed tradition, individual congregations are parts of a broader church community. Just as individual persons are parts of the body of Christ in a congregation, individual congregations are parts of the body of Christ in presbyteries and classes, synods, general assemblies, and the church catholic. Reformed churches sometimes refer to "our connectional system," but this unfortunate term does not express adequately the Reformed understanding of mutual responsibility and accountability among congregations. Congregations are no more self-sufficient than individuals are and, like individuals, are called to use what God has given them for the common good. Congregations that imagine themselves self-sufficient soon become self-absorbed, weakening the body of Christ.

Ordered patterns of ministry and ordered patterns of congregational relationships are ways of ensuring the church's fidelity to the gospel. Although order does not prevent faithlessness, and can become faithless, order in the Reformed tradition is designed to encourage collegial relationships rather than individual autonomy. Reformed polity is an attempt to embody the mutual edification, assistance, and correction that is characteristic of the body *of Christ*.

Today, church order is in danger of conforming to contemporary organizational procedures rather than to the gospel. Pastors often act as CEOs, sessions and consistories conduct business like boards of directors, and deacons are consigned to the performance of undervalued tasks. Presbyteries and classes appear to be consumed by internal institutional affairs, synods have become remote organizations without distinct purpose, and general synods and assemblies act alternately like regulatory agencies or declining companies in search of customers. The church can learn from the insights of organizational theory and group process, but it is not a business, a community service agency, or a government department. Bureaucratic notions of efficiency, profitability, and customer satisfaction are inappropriate substitutes for the gospel in shaping the life of the church. Like every human organization, the church is a body consisting of many parts that must work together. Unlike other organizations, the church is the body of Christ in which the parts are called to work together in Christ's grace, God's love, and the Spirit's communion. The church must hold the gospel at the heart of its ordered life if it is to personify the body of Christ in its patterns of ministry and relationships.

Nevertheless, whatever current faults may swarm within the church, it remains Christ's body, not ours. Because the church is the body of Christ, we can live and work within it, confident of "God's abundant grace toward delinquent churches."[11]

One Holy Catholic Apostolic

The Nicene Creed sets out four marks of the church, four characteristics that identify the shape of its life: *one, holy, catholic, apostolic*. A brief glance at the reality of the church exposes the ambiguity of these marks. How can we confess the church's *oneness* in face of the obvious disunity of the multiple churches that are divided by diverse patterns of faith and life? What does it mean to affirm the church's *holiness* when churches too often conform to the world? Do claims of *catholicity* make sense in light of the church's obvious failures to encompass the wholeness of Christian faith and the wholeness of gender, race, ethnicity, and class? Does *apostolicity* actually characterize churches with a tenuous connection to the apostolic faith and a hesitant commitment to God's mission in the world?

Our confession of the creed may appear to be an empty exercise in religious platitudes. The church's fragmentation, conformity, constriction, and indifference are all too apparent, giving rise to cynicism within the church and continuing rejection by many outside of the church. As we have seen, the common strategy for dealing with the seeming gap between the creed and reality is to acknowledge the failures of the churches while claiming that there is more to *church* than we see. The churches we see are sinful and flawed, but there is a church that we cannot see, and that invisible church is truly and purely what God intends—one holy catholic and apostolic.

The invisibility strategy for maintaining confession of the one holy catholic apostolic church provides easy justification for the present division and constant re-division of the church. The invisibility strategy makes it possible to spurn any flawed congregation or leave any flawed denomination while continuing to claim allegiance to the invisible spiritual reality of the church that is always united, godly, complete, and faithful. The problem, of course, is that the invisible church does not exist within our experience, and so the only option is another flawed church . . . or no church at all. Calvin had little use for people who demand perfect purity and integrity in the church, and so depart from an obviously flawed church. "Indeed," says Calvin, "they are vainly seeking a church besmirched with no blemish."[12] In our time, more and more people abandon the quest.

The invisible church strategy leads to a danger even more perilous than the denigration of actual churches. If the creed's affirmations of the church concern something that exists only in a spiritual realm that is beyond our experience, what of the creed's other affirmations? Do God the Father Almighty, Jesus Christ his only Son our Lord, and the Holy Spirit also exist only in a spiritual realm that is beyond experience? Are creation, crucifixion and resurrection, and one baptism for the forgiveness of sins also abstractions that only hover above the real world? The creed's foundational affirmations of Christian faith are too easily consigned to

an otherworldly realm when the most immediately accessible of its affirmations—
the church—fades into invisibility.

Calvin placed Word and Sacrament at the heart of church life because he was
convinced that they reveal the real presence of Christ with his people. Christ's
presence in the church is not a static existence, for the living Christ continues to
proclaim that God's new Way in the world is at hand, and continues to call us to
repent and believe the gospel, to trust and remain loyal to the good news. Through
Christ, in the power of the Holy Spirit, God *calls* the church to be one, to be holy,
to be catholic, and to be apostolic. The creedal marks are indicative of what *is*
because they are the reality of God's call. The marks of the church are not qualities
inherent in the church's life, but in the life of the church's Lord. The church is
the *ekklesia*, the called community that responds, always with a mixture of faith
and distraction, obedience and rebellion, loyalty and indifference. Yet, because the
church is the body of Christ, the Lord is always present, and his call to be one holy
catholic and apostolic community is always the church's reality.

1. John Updike, *A Month of Sundays* (New York: Alfred A. Knopf, 1975), p. 22.
2. *The Presbyterian Hymnal* (Louisville: Westminster/John Knox Press, 1990), no. 442.
3. Pauw, "The Graced Infirmity of the Church," in *Feminist and Womanist Essays in Reformed Dogmatics*, p. 189.
4. Berkouwer, *The Church*, p. 9.
5. *Institutes*, 4.1.13.
6. Ibid., 4.1.4.
7. Barth, *Dogmatics in Outline* (London: SCM Press, 1949), p. 144.
8. Gerhard Kittel and Gerhard Friedrich, eds., *Theological Dictionary of the New Testament*, vol. 7, (Grand Rapids: Eerdmans, 1971), pp. 1038-1039. See also J. A. T. Robinson, *The Body*, Studies in Biblical Theology, no. 5 (London: SCM, 1952), pp. 59ff.
9. Confession of 1967, 9.32-9.33.
10. *Institutes*, 4.10.30.
11. Ibid., 4.1.27.
12. Ibid., 4.1.13.

10

Justice in an Age
of Self-Interest

"I'm not sure I can take it anymore."
　　*"You can take it. You're the toughest person I've ever seen, Lillian. And as long as you
　　don't worry, you can take it just fine."*
*"I'm not tough. I'm not tough, and I'm not good, and once you get to know me, you'll wish
you'd never set foot in this house."*
　　*"It isn't about goodness. It's about justice, and if justice means anything, it has to be
　　the same for everyone, whether they're good or not."*

Paul Auster, *Leviathan*[1]

Doctrinal disputes that once divided Reformed from Lutheran, Anglican, Catholic,
Methodist, and other churches have receded into the background of church life.
Theological differences among denominations continue to occupy national
church leaders and academic specialists, but they seldom engage ordinary church
members who move freely and comfortably between denominations. Theological
matters are not unimportant, but in contemporary North American churches the
great dividing lines tend to be drawn *within* denominations on matters of ethics
and morals as well as doctrine, on how Christians should act as well as on what
they believe. For most Christians, classical doctrinal and theological matters are
subordinate to moral issues. Few ministers and fewer church members debate
the nature of the real presence of Christ in the Lord's Supper, the doctrine of
the ascension, or the relationship between justification and sanctification. Even
when doctrinal debates occur within denominations, they are more likely to be
argued politically than theologically. For the most part, intra-Christian arguments
are about issues such as abortion, homosexuality, and the appropriate role of the
church in social issues rather than about doctrine. This leads Alan Wolfe to note
that "the strange silence of the Bible in the church" has been joined by "the strange
disappearance of doctrine in the church."[2]

　　Divergent moral and ethical positions do not divide Christians along
denominational lines, for the arguments take place within every denomination.
These internal denominational debates mirror divisions in the society at large,
with little distinction between Christian moral discourse and general discussion
within the culture. The scarcity of discussion on distinctively theological grounds

leads to unresolved Christian disagreements that are too often indistinguishable from unresolved social and political disagreements. Alasdair MacIntyre voices what we all know:

> The most striking feature of contemporary moral utterance is that so much of it is used to express disagreements; and the most striking feature of the debates in which these disagreements are expressed is their interminable character. I do not mean by this just that such debates go on and on and on—although they do—but that they apparently can find no terminus. There seems to be no rational way of securing moral agreement in our culture.[3]

Debates continue in the church as they do throughout society, alienating individuals, splitting congregations, and tearing denominations apart. Just as there seems to be no rational way of securing moral agreement in our culture, there seems to be no faithful way of securing moral agreement in our church.

Division in the church over moral issues goes beyond the presence of diverse views on specific issues, for Christians are unable to share common convictions about how issues should be dealt with and resolved, or what should happen within the community of faith when agreement eludes it. The best that Reformed churches seem able to manage is to fall back on polity, debating and voting in presbyteries, classes, synods, and general assemblies, imagining that a majority vote settles an issue. Of course, our votes rarely settle anything; they are simply skirmishes in a continuing battle. Thus, inconclusive legislative outcomes lead to judicial battles, as one side or the other turns to ecclesiastical courts to adjudicate matters. Judicial decisions are as unpersuasive to the losing side as legislative results. All strategies appear to ensure the "interminable character" of the disputes.

Wide-ranging ecclesial debates about social-ethical issues may not be the church's deepest moral problem. The church's inability to agree upon faithful *corporate* thought and action has confusing consequences for *personal* thought and action. If the community of faith is marked by the absence of shared convictions about the contours of faithful life, where are members of the community to look for guidance and support in shaping their own lives? Abortion, for instance, is not simply—or even primarily—a matter of public policy. Abortion is a possible choice for thousands of persons every day. In the absence of shared Christian convictions about life, mutuality, responsibility, freedom, community, and grace, individuals are thrown back upon their private resources, forced to make lonely choices.

Increasingly, Christian morality, like Christian theology, has become a matter of private opinion. Few Christians long for church laws to govern their every ethical decision. No one is eager for church authorities to tell people what they should or should not do in every instance of moral choice. Yet there is scant comfort if the alternative is ethical anarchy in which each Christian becomes an isolated decision-maker. Is God's Way in the world nothing more than a grant of open permission for individuals to make choices? Or is *God's* Way in the world the gift of new life, the call to a new way of being human within a new human community of faith?

It may be that our ethical impasses are directly related to our neglect of theology. What we believe and how we act are not two distinct things; shared conviction and common action are inseparable within God's new Way in the world. The Presbyterian Church (U.S.A.)'s Historic Principles of Church Order assert, "That truth is in order to goodness . . . . We are persuaded that there is an inseparable connection between faith and practice, truth and duty. Otherwise, it would be of no consequence either to discover truth or to embrace it."[4] Thinking about the faith (theology) shapes the way faithful women and men live (morality) just as the way faithful people live affects their thinking about the faith. Thinking and acting are inseparable. Moreover, *Christian* thinking and acting are properly lodged within the *community* of faith, not merely inside of each person, in isolation from brothers and sisters. That is the problem we face: There is no agreement within the church, and therefore little guidance for the faithful who must give shape to their lives each day.

Christian Freedom

"For freedom Christ has set us free," says Paul (Galatians 5:1). The freedom of Christians is not a generalized exemption from all restriction, but a hallmark of our justification by grace through faith. Freedom in Christ is our emancipation from enslavement to the "principalities and powers"—the ideologies, institutions, and images that tell us who we are and how we are to live. Christ frees us from conformity to cultural values and societal projects; Christ frees us for new life within God's good Way. "You will know the truth, and the truth will make you free" (John 8:32) is more than a motto chiseled over library entrances; it is a proclamation of the gospel. Readers of John's Gospel are not stuck with Pilate's question—"What is truth?"—for by the time in the narrative that the question is asked, readers have already encountered the bold declaration that *Jesus Christ* is "the way, and the *truth,* and the life" (John 14:6). The freedom of Christians comes from knowing Christ, and the freedom of Christians is lived by hearing Christ's call and following where Christ leads.

For Calvin, as for Luther before him, Christian freedom was at the heart of the gospel. "Unless this freedom be comprehended," he wrote, "neither Christ nor gospel truth, nor inner peace of soul, can rightly be known."[5] Freedom in Christ is the good news of emancipation from slavish duty, the proclamation "that the consciences of believers, in seeking their justification before God, should rise above and advance beyond the law, forgetting all law righteousness . . . We should, when justification is being discussed, embrace God's mercy alone, turn our attention from ourselves, and look only to Christ."[6] Neither obedience to the law nor conformity to rules and customs wins God's favor. In Christ, we are set free from constant striving to be "good enough," free to turn away from anxious introspection, free to turn toward Christ and the certainty of *God's* righteousness.

Liberation from nervous striving to justify ourselves before God seems to be a Protestant commonplace, but contemporary church life is replete with instances of seeking to establish righteousness by adherence to laws. The Ten Commandments may suffer from neglect, but in some church circles the quality of faith, indeed faith itself, is gauged by compliance to more recent rules and regulations. Groups within the church establish "correct" positions on gender-inclusive language, or the inspiration of the Bible, or the ordination of gay and lesbian persons, or abortion, or same-sex marriage, or a host of other matters. Woe to those whose views depart from prevailing orthodoxies! *Real* Christians use inclusive language (or insist on the male metaphors and pronouns of the Bible); believe that God inspired every word in the Bible (or that the Scriptures are human words); oppose the ordination of self-avowed, practicing homosexual persons (or favor it); uphold a woman's right to control her body (or condemn abortion as murder); confine marriage to the union of one man and one woman (or include same-sex couples in marriage). In all of this, people may worry less about meriting God's favor than being on the right side of a moral issue, but the effect is the same: Adherence to standards becomes the mark of righteousness.

Calvin was an astute observer of human thought and behavior, and so he recognized that any form of "works righteousness" turns our attention away from Christ and toward ourselves. As we attempt to defend our goodness, the grace of the Lord Jesus Christ, the love of God, and the communion of the Holy Spirit are quickly replaced by preoccupation with proper observance of rules and constant concern about the extent of our adherence to norms. Knowing the rules and following them become essential to winning the approval of others, if not of God. If our worth is based on knowing the rules and obeying them, we soon become enmeshed in a web of anxiety that chokes freedom: Do we know all the rules? Do we interpret them properly? Do we observe them adequately? "For freedom Christ has set us free," says Paul. "Stand firm, therefore, and do not submit again to a yoke of slavery" (Galatians 5:1). Striving to prove our worth by meeting normative standards is a form of the captivity from which Christ has freed us.

Freedom is not license, however. In a North American culture that prizes freedom, including freedom from "outmoded" ethical and moral norms, we may need to be reminded that Christian freedom from bondage to law is freedom for living God's Way in the world, for doing God's will. "The second part [of

Christian freedom], dependent upon the first," says Calvin, "is that consciences observe the law, not as if constrained by the necessity of the law, but that freed from the law's yoke they willingly obey God's will."[7] The freedom Christ gives is not permission to do whatever we please; Christ frees us to hear God's call and follow in God's Way. Because God is love, and love seeks the well-being of the beloved, God's loving will for human life has form and content. God is not indifferent to us, unconcerned about the direction of our lives. We are free from the obligation of compliance to laws, but not cut loose from the love of God.

Calvin likens the distinction between obeying rules for their own sake and living freely in God's Way to the difference between master-servant and parent-child relationships. Masters give orders to their servants, assigning tasks that must be fulfilled. The dynamic of every master-servant relationship is compulsion, and the servant's "freedom" is limited to the freedom to fail. Unlike masters, parents who love their children do not issue orders and compel obedience. Parents try to give direction to children's lives, of course. They guide and correct, make rules and exercise discipline. Parents' expectations grow from loving concern for their children's well-being, not from the sheer exercise of parental dominance. Thus, children are free to respond in love rather than fear. "Such children ought we to be," says Calvin, "firmly trusting that our services will be approved by our most merciful Father, however small, rude, and imperfect these may be."[8] In freedom, our attention is turned away from ourselves and from our anxious striving. Our attention is turned toward God, whose attention is lovingly fixed upon us!

Christian freedom from fretful obedience to laws and rules makes us capable of joyful obedience to God's good will for human life. Obedience to God does not mire us in a bog of minute details. For Calvin, the third aspect of Christian freedom involves the recognition that some of the choices we make have no clear right and wrong. We are free to do or not do certain things, to act or not act in certain ways, for these things are "indifferent" (Latin: *adiaphora*). Unless we realize that we have latitude within God's Way, we will find ourselves in "a long and inextricable maze, not easy to get out of."[9] God's good will for human life is not a complex code that we must decipher or a blueprint we must follow. Seeing everything in terms of right or wrong diverts our eyes from Christ, turning our gaze upon ourselves and upon the imagined extent of our scrupulous obedience.

Reformed Christians have always known that confession of sin is a constant necessity. However, confession is not an anxious cataloging of grand and petty wrongs, but rather a candid acknowledgment of our self-deception, our self-assertion, and our self-generated distance from God. Moreover, confession of sin is not made to ensure forgiveness, as if our declaration of guilt produces a declaration of pardon. Sin is acknowledged honestly, with the certain confidence that in Christ God has forgiven us and renews the presence among us of the Spirit of truth who will guide us into all truth (John 16:13). Thus, we do not confess sin *in order* to be forgiven; we confess sin because we know that *we are* forgiven and because confession of sin is a necessary element in repentance—the turning away from sin and turning toward God's new Way in the world.

How do we discern the shape of God's new Way in the world? How are we to escape the snares of self-deception? The conclusion of Calvin's confession liturgy is the recitation of the Law—the Decalogue—as the God-given shape of life for a redeemed people. While the Reformed tradition has always understood that the Law convicts of sin and deters social wrongs, it has emphasized Calvin's positive assessment of the Law's place in the life of faith:

> The third and principal use, which pertains more closely to the proper purpose of the law, finds its place among believers in whose hearts the Spirit of God already lives and reigns. . . . Here is the best instrument for them to learn more thoroughly each day the nature of the Lord's will to which they aspire, and to confirm them in the understanding of it. . . . For no man has heretofore attained to such wisdom as to be unable, from the daily instruction of the law, to make fresh progress toward a purer knowledge of the divine will.[10]

This positive use of the Law found expression in Calvin's confession liturgy, for the Decalogue *followed* the prayer of confession and the declaration of pardon. Instead of pointing an accusing finger, the Law points the way to new life that can be lived in the fullness of communion with God and neighbors. That is why Calvin's congregations in Strasbourg and Geneva sang the Ten Commandments. Repentance, which begins with confession of sin, is completed in grateful embrace of the revealed will of God.

Christian liberty is freedom *from* laws, rules, and regulations; freedom *for* living God's Way in the world; freedom *to* discern that some things are central to Christian living while other things are not. Does this really help us? While Calvin may lead us to appreciate our liberation from conformity to social norms and churchly laws, how are we to know the will of God? How are we to determine what is at the heart of God's Way? How can we know, in any given instance, what to do? Even if we agree that God's law is a good gift, setting forth the shape of good life for a redeemed people, how do we decide what the law requires? "You shall not murder" (Exodus 20:13) is God's good will for faithful living, but does it help us know what to do when faced with social and personal matters such as capital punishment, abortion, euthanasia, terrorism, and war? Are we not thrown back into the arenas of interminable church debate and lonely private choice?

Theological Ethics

Neither endless church argument nor isolated personal option is the necessary outcome of Christian freedom. Perhaps we can discern the outline of both social and personal ethics in a twentieth-century episode in the church's history. In 1934, the church in Germany was confronted with Nazi attempts to control its faith and life. In the face of the real danger that the church would allow itself to become subservient to National Socialism, representatives of Reformed, Lutheran, and United churches met in the small city of Barmen and agreed upon a theological declaration of the faith. Although the declaration was occasioned by Nazi totalitarianism, its affirmation of Christian faith transcends limited time and place. The Presbyterian Church (U.S.A.) includes the Theological Declaration of Barmen in its *Book of Confessions* as a valuable guide to contemporary Christian faith and life.

The Barmen Declaration is notable for what it says *no* to as well as what it says *yes* to, coupling six "evangelical truths" with a denial of six "errors." Both the affirmations and the denials provide the church and its members with an approach to faith and life that is neither privatistic nor legalistic, neither idiosyncratic nor conformist. The issue in Germany in the 1930s was moral and urgent: How should the church—its ministers and members—respond to the Nazi attempt to co-opt the church for its own purposes? Although the question at Barmen was unusually dramatic, the necessity of choice is commonplace for Christian communities and their members. Persons, congregations, and denominations are faced regularly with situations and issues that call upon us to decide who we are and how we are to live. On what basis do we decide? Barmen begins by declaring that the ground of our judgment must be theological—that is, grounded in the gospel and in service of God's new Way in the world:

> [1] Jesus Christ, as he is attested for us in Holy Scripture, is the one Word of God which we have to hear and which we have to trust and obey in life and in death.
>
> We reject the false doctrine, as though the church could and would have to acknowledge as a source of its proclamation, apart from and besides this one Word of God, still other events and powers, figures and truths, as God's revelation.[11]

No shortage of "events and powers, figures and truths" attempts to tell us what to believe and how to live. Businesses, schools, government, and the media all proclaim "values" that shape public perceptions, choices, and actions. The cultural realities within which people live may be as obviously evil as Nazi Germany or seem as benign as contemporary America, but in either case social arrangements and cultural assumptions are proclaimed in subtle, taken-for-granted ways. The companies we work for, the television shows we watch, the advertising we hear and see, the neighborhoods we live in, the books we read, and the Internet sites we visit—indeed, every facet of our culture—embody assumptions about what is true and desirable. We breathe a social and cultural atmosphere that seldom captures our conscious attention because it is, quite simply, "the way things are."

Most Christians would affirm that Jesus Christ is "the one Word which we have to hear, trust, and obey," but this can become a cliché unless it is accompanied by awareness of the competing words spoken by the culture. The sounds of our culture are like background music; most of the time we are barely aware of the tune. We may find ourselves singing the culture's songs, assuming that they are in harmony with the hymns of Christian faith. We may even come to identify congenial social realities with the gospel, not even realizing that our understanding of what is Christian has become shaped as much by social class or political preference as by the one Word of God. Kevin Vanhoozer notes, "Disciples do not follow the gospel in a vacuum, but wend their Christian way through particular times and places, each with its own problems and possibilities. We can follow God's word only if we know where we are and have a sense of where various ways lead."[12] The culture in which we live is neither uniformly evil nor wholly good, but unless we are aware of both its overt and hidden messages, we will be passive consumers of its offerings. Christians are not called to escape from "the world" or to accept its every norm, convention, and fashion. Christians are called to hear the one Word of God, and to test every other word by what they hear in Jesus Christ.

Community Ethics

Christian morality begins with Christian theology—faithful listening for the one Word of God accompanied by critical attention to the words of other events and powers, figures and truths that vie for our attention and acquiescence. Yet it is not easy to hear the one Word of God while our ears are being assaulted by the stereophonic *babel* of the culture. Thus, Barmen also declares that listening for the one Word of God is the responsibility of Christians together; ethical judgments begin with the *community* of faith:

> [3] The Christian Church is the congregation of the brethren in which Jesus Christ acts presently as the Lord in Word and Sacrament through the Holy Spirit. As the church of pardoned sinners, it has to testify in the midst of a sinful world, with its faith as with its obedience, with its message as with its order, that it is solely his property, and that it lives and wants to live solely from his comfort and from his direction in the expectation of his appearance.

We reject the false doctrine, as though the church were permitted to abandon the form of its message and order to its own pleasure or to changes in prevailing ideological and political convictions.[13]

The one Word of God to whom we listen is not a faint voice from the distant past, but a living presence. The risen Christ is among us now in the power of the Holy Spirit. Among *us* now, for the primary presence of Christ is with the community of faith, the church. Thus, in seeking the will of God each of us stands with sisters and brothers, listening together for God's Word and seeking God's will. This does not mean that individuals should abdicate responsibility to the institutional church, of course, but it does mean that ears and voices can be joined in a common quest for faithful obedience to God. Neither does it mean that individuals must lose themselves in conformity to groupthink, but it does mean that mutual listening, questioning, talking, and praying can free us from the unconscious seductions of self-direction. It is in "the congregation of the brethren" that Jesus Christ acts presently as Lord, says Barmen, so that the faithful may live from Christ's comfort and direction rather than from their own pleasure or from prevailing cultural preferences.

How do we know God's good will for human life, for our own lives? How do we decide when faced with choices about who we shall be and how we shall live? There are no Christian formulas, but our asking and deciding do not take place in a vacuum. We are not alone. God is with us, and our brothers and sisters in faith are with us.

Since *God* is with us, our ethical decisions begin with God and God's Way in the world. Our faith in God—our beliefs about God, our trust in God's love, our loyalty to God's Way—is the foundation of our life. Without the right foundation, the rest of the structure is arbitrary and will not stand for long. How can we expect to know what God calls us to be and do if we fail to inquire about the reality of God and God's Way among us?

Since our *sisters and brothers* are with us, we are not solitary ethical agents. Each of us makes decisions that shape who we are and how we live. The daily flow of life in our families, neighborhoods, schools, and jobs presents us with occasions to be one kind of person or another, to act this way or that way. Most of the time we do not make conscious, explicit choices; we simply are who we are. The good news of the gospel is that we are who we are "in Christ." Our very identity is no longer determined by our past or dictated by the present. Being in Christ creates a new reality so distinct that it can be expressed only by the image of new birth. "So if anyone is in Christ," says Paul, "there is a new creation: everything old has passed away; see, everything has become new!" (2 Corinthians 5:17). We are new men and women in Christ; Christ forms new character in us, develops new virtues in us, creates new habits of the heart in us.

Being in Christ is being in the body of Christ, the community of faith, the church. Like-mindedness does not form this community of faith in Christ nor is it maintained by superficial agreement or smooth tolerance. The community is called into being by Christ, given its character by Christ, and sustained by Christ. Thus, our character, virtues, and habits of the heart are shaped within the body of Christ. We do not have to rely on the self-help industry to make us whole, for we have the gift of sisters and brothers who, with us, seek to have "the same mind . . . that was in Christ Jesus" (Philippians 2:5). As we share life in Christ, we grow together in Christ, helping each other develop distinctive Christian character and sustained Christian virtues that form a Christian ethic among us. Ethical dilemmas persist, of course, but we need not face them in isolation from our faith or from other believers. Even when we face the most excruciating decisions, we are not alone; we remain in the body of Christ, with Christ and with Christ's people.

Let Justice Roll Down

The subtle seductions of our culture, our moral privatism, and the interminable character of ethical argument in the church are all apparent when Christians talk about justice. In American society, justice is achieved through the adversarial assertion of competing rights. Individuals and groups have rights, we say, and justice is achieved when law secures these rights. Since different rights may be in conflict, competing claims must be adjudicated through the legal system. From civil rights to the right of privacy, from the right to life through the right to die, it seems that every group and every person is sheathed in an armor of rights. This understanding of justice may be a good and necessary feature of American democracy (although it requires that well over half of the world's lawyers practice in the United States!). Is the assertion of competing rights what Amos had in mind when he called for justice to roll down like waters and righteousness like an ever-flowing stream?

Framing Christian ethical discussion with categories of rights guarantees that endless disagreement will ensue. Formulating the issue of abortion as either the rights of the unborn or the right of a woman to control her own body is a recipe for perpetual disagreement. Confining the church's discussion of homosexuality to the individual's right to be ordained, or the presbytery's right to ordain whoever it wishes, or the General Assembly's right to issue definitive guidance and authoritative interpretation of who may be ordained, ensures that legal compulsion will be the only available resolution. When the church absorbs the culture's equation of justice with rights, it not only accepts the inevitability of adversarial relationships, but it consigns each of its members to the realm of private, subjective decision. *Self*-interest becomes the norm within the church as in the society.

The good news of God's justice is *shalom*, the wholeness of new human relationships within the grace of God. God's justice is the presence of personal and communal life that shares in the goodness of creation, enjoying life together with God and with other people. Perhaps we can begin to appreciate the fullness of God's justice when we realize that the Greek word for "justice," *dikaiosune*, is usually translated "righteousness" within the New Testament. "Blessed are those who hunger and thirst for *dikaiosune* [justice/righteousness]" is not an invitation to assert rights, but to enjoy the fullness of loving relationship with God and with all neighbors. Justice (right relationship) is both a personal and social goal that the church can pursue within the community of faith and throughout the human community. As it does, the church can live in freedom from battles over conflicting rights, in freedom for God's Way of *shalom* in the world, in freedom to hear and follow Christ's call.

Yes and No

Genuine confession of faith, and genuine judgments about the shape of faithful living, always entails both affirmation of truth and denial of untruth. Christian community and Christian discipleship require renunciation of what is not from God as well as affirmation of God and of God's Way. Sometimes the *no* is explicit, as with Barmen and the Confession of 1967; at other times it is implicit, as with the Nicene and Apostles' creeds. As the church and its members strive to define themselves in fidelity to the grace of the Lord Jesus Christ, the love of God, and the communion of the Holy Spirit, they must say *yes* to their perception of God's Way in the world, and *no* to the ways of the world apart from God. "If the Yes does not in some way contain the No," said Karl Barth, "it will not be the Yes of a confession. . . . If we have not the confidence to say *damnamus* [what we refuse], then we might as well omit the *credimus* [what we believe]."[14]

It may be tempting to think that our confession of faith (theology) is the positive pole while our moral teaching (ethics) is the negative pole. We state our beliefs positively ("We believe in one God, the Father, the Almighty . . . We believe in one Lord Jesus Christ, the only Son of God . . . We believe in the Holy Spirit, the Lord, the giver of life"), while we express our behavioral norms negatively ("You shall not murder . . . you shall not commit adultery . . . you shall not steal . . . you shall not bear false witness . . . you shall not covet"). As we confess the Nicene Creed, we are saying *no* to the monistic deity of bourgeois religiosity by proclaiming Holy Trinity. Similarly, when we say that we will not steal, we are saying *yes* to a way of life that encompasses the widest range of personal relationships, communal interactions, and social justice. The Reformed understanding of our ethical and moral yes is most evident in catechisms—dialogues on faith and life. Reformed catechisms always deal with the Apostles' Creed, the Ten Commandments, and the Lord's Prayer. They also follow a pattern of asking what each commandment requires of us before asking what each commandment prohibits.

The Westminster Larger Catechism—perhaps the least inviting of the documents in the *Book of Confessions*—presents a remarkable portrait of personal and societal life lived in God's Way. What does the Larger Catechism say that the commandment "You shall not steal" requires of us? In part:

> truth, faithfulness, and justice in contracts and commerce . . . rendering to everyone his due . . . giving and lending freely, according to our abilities, and the necessities of others; moderation of our judgments, wills, and affections, concerning worldly goods . . . a lawful calling, and a diligence in it; frugality; avoiding unnecessary lawsuits . . . and an endeavor by all just and lawful means to procure, preserve, and further the wealth and outward estate of others, as well as our own.[15]

The *no* contains the *yes!* The prohibition against stealing contains the affirmative obligation to work for the well-being of others, throughout society as well as in personal relationships. Similarly, the contemporary *Study Catechism*, approved by the Presbyterian Church (U.S.A.) in 1998, asks what we learn from the sixth commandment, "You shall not murder":

> God forbids anything that harms my neighbor unfairly. Murder or injury can be done not only by direct violence but also by an angry word or a clever plan, and not only by an individual but also by unjust social institutions. I should honor every human being, including my enemy, as a person made in God's image.[16]

The *negative* contains the *positive!* The seemingly straightforward prohibition of murder contains the affirmative obligation to honor all people, working for the establishment and maintenance of just social institutions. From the sixteenth century on, churches of the Reformed tradition have taught that the establishment of justice—the harmonious ordering of all personal and social relationships—is the necessary task of the people who know God's grace, love, and communion.

The Confession of 1967 includes a section on "Reconciliation in Society." The confession affirms that God calls the church to act in response to specific problems and crises. In particular times and places, then, "the church, guided by the Spirit, humbled by its own complicity and instructed by all attainable knowledge, seeks to discern the will of God and learn how to obey in these concrete situations."[17] C'67 lifts up four urgent issues—racial discrimination, threats to international peace, poverty, and anarchy in sexual relationships. The same issues remain forty years later, although their specific shape has changed. Perhaps more important than the confession's precise expressions of the four issues is the way that it articulates dangers to the church's faithfulness:

> Congregations, individuals, or groups of Christians who exclude, dominate, or patronize others, however subtly, resist the Spirit of God and bring contempt on the faith which they profess. . . .
>
> Although nations may serve God's purpose in history, the church which identifies the sovereignty of any one nation or any one way of life with the cause of God denies the Lordship of Christ and betrays its calling. . . .
>
> A church that is indifferent to poverty, or evades responsibility in economic affairs, or is open to one social class only, or expects gratitude for its beneficence makes a mockery of reconciliation and offers no acceptable worship to God. . . .
>
> The church comes under the judgment of God and invites rejection by society when it fails to lead men and women into the full meaning of life together, or withholds the compassion of Christ from those caught in the moral confusion of our time.[18]

These confessional *nos* are addressed to us, to the shape of our ecclesial and personal Christian life. The confession is less interested in the church presuming to tell the world how it should act than in reminding Christians of our calls to live God's new Way in the world. This does not mean that the church is indifferent to the common good. Far from it, for the church is sent into the world as God's reconciling community to work for an end to racial and ethnic injustices, to strive for peace, to promote policies that overcome poverty and provide economic opportunity, and to oppose the degradations of an exploitative culture. However, the church does not call for societal justice as if it were innocent of the evils it condemns. Before it tells the world what to do, the church and its members must plumb the depths of Christian complicity in the world's injustices.

Additional insight comes from the Confession of Belhar, written in South Africa during the apartheid era, and now the confessional basis of the Uniting Reformed Church and the Uniting Presbyterian Church in South Africa, and in the process of becoming a confessional standard for the Reformed Church in America, the Christian Reformed Church, and the Presbyterian Church (U.S.A.). This Reformed confession gets the matter right: *God* is the author of justice and peace; the church is called to *follow* God in the ways of justice and peace. Belhar affirms that God "brings justice to the oppressed and gives bread to the hungry . . . frees the prisoner and restores sight to the blind . . . supports the downtrodden, protects the stranger, helps orphans and widows and blocks the path of the ungodly." Belhar also affirms, "The church as the possession of God must stand where the Lord stands."[19]

As the possession of God, the church and all individual believers are freed from captivity within the web of society's injustices, and freed from the straitjacket of competing rights. As the possession of God, the church and all believers are free to stand where God stands, and to follow in God's Way of *shalom*.

1. Auster, *Leviathan*, p. 232.
2. Alan Wolfe, *The Transformation of American Religion: How We Actually Live Our Faith* (New York: Free Press, 2002), p. 3.
3. Alasdair MacIntyre, *After Virtue*, 2nd ed. (Notre Dame: University of Notre Dame Press, 1984), p. 6.
4. *Book of Order*, G-1.0304.
5. *Institutes*, 3.19.1., p. 834.
6. Ibid., 3.19.2., p. 834.
7. Ibid., 3.19.4., p. 836.
8. Ibid., 3.19.5., p. 837.
9. Ibid., 3.19.7., p. 839.
10. Ibid., 2.7.12., p. 360.
11. Theological Declaration of Barmen, *Book of Confessions*, 8.11–8.12.
12. Kevin Vanhoozer, ed., *Everyday Theology: How to Read Cultural Texts and Interpret Trends* (Grand Rapids: Baker Academic, 2007), p. 16.
13. The Theological Declaration of Barmen, 8.17–8.18.
14. Barth, *Church Dogmatics*, I/2, pp. 631, 630.
15. The Larger Catechism, *Book of Confessions*, 7.251.
16. *Study Catechism: Full Version* (Louisville: Witherspoon Press, 1998), p. 64.
17. Confession of 1967, *Book of Confessions*, 9.43.
18. Ibid., 9.44–9.47.
19. Confession of Belhar, images.rca.org/docs/aboutus/belharconfession.pdf, p. 5.

11

A Missional Postscript

The first Christians he met as a boy in Korea were Adventist missionaries, very simple people. They had no power and wanted no power. They told us Bible stories, it is true. But they gave us food and shelter and medicine first, and teased us and told us jokes and played with us and loved us. So we begged them for the stories. . . . This was what Joon thought Christianity meant! Food and medicine for the body, and stories for the heart if you begged for them. Then he came here, found a country full of people begging not to hear the stories, went to seminary, and found out why. No food. No medicine. No doing unto others. Just a bunch of men learning how to bellow the stories at others whether they wanted to hear them or not!

David James Duncan, *The Brothers K*[1]

Mission once conjured up images of people sent to far corners of the world to preach the gospel, calling persons to Christian faith. "Foreign missionaries" proclaimed the good news of God's grace in Jesus Christ, establishing churches, schools, and hospitals. They provided agricultural assistance, operated orphanages, and gave hundreds of languages their first written form. Although it is fashionable in some church circles to denigrate this missionary movement, charging it with cultural imperialism, the reality is that it drew millions into vibrant faith and led to the formation of vital churches throughout Africa, Asia, and Latin America. Today, a majority of the world's Christians live in former "mission fields," and the dynamism of their churches contrasts with the diminution and lethargy of much European and North American church life.

The popular narrative of Protestant missions goes something like this: The sixteenth-century Reformers had little if any missionary consciousness and their lack of awareness carried over into the age of Protestant Orthodoxy. The Catholic Church carried out what missionary activity could be found in the world. It was not until the emergence of Protestant Pietism in the late eighteenth and early nineteenth century that the great missionary age began. The nineteenth and early twentieth century witnessed remarkable worldwide activity, first by missionary societies, then by the churches themselves. Missionary movements helped to foster ecumenical cooperation among the churches, epitomized by the great 1910 World Missionary Conference in Edinburgh. Edinburgh may have been the high-water mark of missionary endeavor, however, for critique of the missionary movement accelerated, leading to a weakening of the churches' commitment. As commitment to international mission declined, the distinction between what the church did within its own life (ministry) and what it did beyond itself (mission) collapsed as everything the church did came to be called mission. Only now, the story goes, is recovery of the church's genuinely "missional" nature taking place.

Like all popular narratives, there is enough truth to keep the story going but more than enough simplification to distort reality. It may be worth a brief look at the past to ask whether the Reformed tradition has theological and ecclesial resources that can inform our understanding of the missional task facing the church today.

Mission in Geneva?

Lutheran theologian Carl Braaten claims, "The problem of a Protestant theology of mission is that its classical sources, the theology of the Reformers and the confessional writings, are totally devoid of any missionary consciousness."[2] His judgment may be too harsh. It is true enough that missional vocabulary did not flow naturally from Calvin's pen. He lived within the bounds of Christendom, assuming that Christianity was the proper order of society and culture as well as of the church. But Calvin also assumed that something had gone wrong in Christendom, both in the church and in late medieval society and culture. Like Luther and Zwingli before him, he saw his task as reform of the church and the consequent transformation of society.

Viewing the North American church at the beginning of the twenty-first century, missional theologian Darrell Guder declares,

> The church's crisis is one of fundamental vocation, of calling to God's mission, of being, doing, and saying witness in faithfulness to Jesus Christ, the Lord. Our missional challenge is a crisis of faith and spirit, and it will be met only through conversion, the continuing conversion of the church.[3]

Guder's analysis of the challenge facing the church is not altogether different from that of the reformers; the continuing conversion of the church was also a sixteenth-century aim. When Calvin responded to Catholic critics by justifying the necessity of church reform his rationale was consistent. Negatively, he contended that "the question is not whether the Church suffers from many and grievous diseases, for this is admitted even by all moderate judges; but whether the diseases are of a kind whose cure admits of no longer delay."[4] Positively, he proclaimed,

Our writings are witnesses, and our sermons also, how frequent and sedulous we are in recommending true repentance . . . that [all] may be brought into obedience to God alone, and look no longer to themselves but to him. Nor indeed do we overlook external duties and works of charity, which follow on such renewal.[5]

The mission of the reformers, and the mission of their churches, was to call the whole church to faithfulness in the love of God and neighbors. This necessitated the church's conversion, the reordering of its life, and the reorientation of its role in society.

Calvin's mission in Geneva was not restricted to reform of the church. In an age when the bounds of the church and the society were virtually identical, Calvin labored to make the city a model community that would show forth the light of the gospel. He understood the distinction between church and civil government, but he also understood that Christian life was not confined to the internal life of the church. Ronald Wallace's study of Calvin as social reformer and churchman notes Calvin's conviction that "the individual of his day should not only find salvation by faith in Jesus Christ, but should also discern that he mattered in the community . . . and that his own contribution to the social group was of value."[6] Christian presence in the social order was not limited to the vocation of individuals, however, for Calvin aimed "to create at the heart of the city a community of the faithful in Christ whose ways of mutual forbearance, love and forgiveness would provide a pattern for the rest of civil society."[7] The life of each Christian and the life of the church were to provide clear testimony to the gospel, but Christian witness was to extend beyond personal and inner-church life. The church was to be engaged in social and political life, working to bring about a compassionate and just social order, for reform was not only an intramural church matter. "We remain unworthy to look upon heaven," Calvin wrote, "until there is harmony and unanimity in religion, till God is purely worshiped by all, and all the world is reformed."[8]

Calvin preached, wrote, and lobbied for social improvements ranging from public education and medical care to the construction of a sewer system and the development of a more economical cooking stove for the poor. Through Calvin's leadership, Geneva became a haven for refugees and immigrants from countries throughout Europe and beyond. From Geneva, many went back to France, the Netherlands, England and Scotland, Poland, Italy, Hungary, and beyond, working for the "continuing conversion" of the church. Calvin provided encouragement and support for the churches in those countries, with particular concern for the beleaguered churches in France. Calvin's deep relationship with the Reformed churches in France also involved him in a brief, unsuccessful attempt at mission in South America.

Calvin's tireless labor for the conversion of the church and the establishment of a just society challenges the church in our time to understand the nature of its mission to its own society. Health care, educational opportunity, and welcome of immigrants and refugees are matters that are as pressing for twenty-first-century American churches as they were for the church in sixteenth-century Geneva. "Mission" was not a nineteenth-century Protestant invention, and "missional" is not a twentieth-century innovation. Some of the missional challenges of our time and place can be met with resources that have deep roots in the Reformed tradition.

The End of Christendom

Church and society were virtually coterminous in the sixteenth century, with the church enjoying privileged status and state support. The situation in twenty-first-century North America is radically different. There was a time when the religious life of the United States was characterized by "mainline" Protestant churches. The designation "mainline" included the denominations that developed from the sixteenth-century Protestant Reformation: English Puritans and other independents in New England, Dutch Reformed in New York and New Jersey, Anglicans in Virginia, Scotch-Irish Presbyterians in Pennsylvania and the Carolinas. These are the groups that became the Congregationalists, Presbyterians, Reformed, Episcopalians, and (later) Methodists. They dominated the religious, civic, and cultural life of the United States for three hundred and fifty years.

Historically, Presbyterians, Episcopalians, and Congregationalists were the elite mainline churches. They were influential out of proportion to their numbers, overrepresented among presidents, members of Congress, Supreme Court justices, and judges. Together with the Dutch Reformed, Presbyterians and Episcopalians were prominent in industry and finance. Presbyterian Calvinist values deeply influenced American education.

Now, the mainline churches are in decline—in numbers, but more significantly in eminence and influence. Sociologists and cultural commentators now refer to them as "sideline," "oldline," and "offline" churches. There have been three distinct phases in the progressive disestablishment of the church in North America: legal disestablishment in the eighteenth century, civic disestablishment in the nineteenth century, and cultural disestablishment in the twentieth century.

Legal Disestablishment

Some of the original British colonies embraced the European pattern of state-sanctioned and state-supported churches. Puritans in Massachusetts and Anglicans in Virginia, along with others, institutionalized the ecclesiastical affiliations of the majority. There were protests against state churches from the outset, however, and legal disestablishment was well under way in the colonies by the time of the revolution. Independence from English rule was accompanied by independence from religious hegemony as "separation of church and state" was embedded in the new republic's Bill of Rights.

Civic Disestablishment

Legal disestablishment of the churches did not abolish the standing of the churches in American society, however. It left intact the social and civic dominance of the mainline Congregational, Presbyterian, and Episcopalian churches—together with the Reformed and Methodists. This preeminence was soon to weaken as waves of immigration throughout the nineteenth century brought other religious groups to the United States. Irish, Italian, and Eastern European Catholics and Jews from throughout Europe joined German and Scandinavian Lutherans.

The proliferation of churches was broadened by the emergence of American-born denominations such as the Disciples of Christ and numerous free and holiness churches, as well as the Mormons and other non-Christian groups. All of this led to the civic disestablishment of all churches, but especially of the old mainline. Since no church or family of churches was the majority church, none could be granted civic dominance; all churches were immersed in the new reality of Christian pluralism.

Cultural Disestablishment

Legal disestablishment took place early in the nation's history, at a time when state churches remained the norm in Europe. Civic disestablishment then broke the residual hegemony of the founding churches. Through all of this, however, a generalized cultural establishment of the churches endured. The United States remained a "Christian nation." Conceptual, social, and cultural establishment endured long after legal and civic establishments were only memories; Christianity and Americanism were merged in a unified national religiosity. Christianity helped to shape American optimism and pragmatism while America's version of modernity helped to shape the churches. This symbiotic relationship strengthened the nation and rewarded the churches. Although there were no formally established churches, and although no one church enjoyed exclusive civic dominance, Christianity was the favored religion of the society. Canadian theologian Douglas John Hall identifies this cultural establishment as "part and parcel of our whole inherited 'system of meaning,' a system intermingling Judeo-Christian, Enlightenment, Romantic-idealist, and more recently nationalistic elements."[9]

The post-World War II decades were tumultuous times. Virulent anti-communism, the civil rights movement, Vietnam, the struggle for women's rights, the sexual revolution, Watergate, and more led to a diffusion of the prevailing national purpose. The blurring of national vision hastened the culture's movement away from the moral articulators of that vision—the churches. During the second half of the twentieth century, the churches became effectively distanced from the dominant culture. By the end of the century, the old mainline churches were marginalized, previously marginal evangelical churches were reluctant and ineffective social players, and religion generally was relegated to private life. The decades from 1960 to 2000 saw the rapidly accelerating cultural disestablishment of the churches.

The growing distance between North American culture and the church, and especially the old mainline churches, is evident in numerous quantifiable ways. Mainline Protestant churches have experienced precipitous declines in membership, while the Catholic Church's stream of religious vocations has dried to a trickle. The large network of church-related colleges and universities has been weakened as schools distance themselves from denominational identification. News coverage of religion constricts while entertainment media have replaced stock treatment of religious themes and characters with dismissive characterizations of Christianity and fascination with the occult.

More telling than the sum of specific indicators, however, is the dramatic shift in public attitudes toward Christianity and its churches. Simply put, Christianity is no longer conspicuous in American consciousness and its churches are no longer integral to American culture. The reasons for the cultural disestablishment of the church are complex, the product of multiple forces over long periods. Nevertheless, the reality of cultural disestablishment is a noticeable feature of the contemporary North American religious landscape. Now Christianity is but one of the many religious communities that have found a home here and it is no longer accorded special status in American culture. The church is only one of a profusion of religious options ranging from enduring traditions such as Islam, Buddhism, and Hinduism to New Age spiritualities. Increasingly, Americans see themselves as "spiritual, but not religious."

The legal, civic, and cultural disestablishment of the church is the context within which a North American missional theology is developing. *Missional* is a recently coined term that is too often used (and misused) loosely to cover a wide range of approaches and activities. In spite of this fluidity, missional theology can be characterized by three central convictions. First, mission is not primarily an activity of the church, but a characteristic of God's movement toward the world. The *missio Dei*—mission of God—is, primarily, the Father's sending of the Son in the power of the Spirit and then, derivatively, the church's participation in God's mission. Second, it follows that the church is not the body that sends people into mission, but rather the body that God sends into mission. A third feature of missional thinking is that mission does not occur only "there," but also "here." Since God loves the whole world, the whole world, including the part we inhabit, is within the scope of the *missio Dei*. North America is a mission field into which God sends the church.

Missio Dei

The current shift in missional thinking is often traced to an address given by Karl Barth to the Brandenburg Missionary Conference in 1932. In this address, Barth articulated the proposition that mission is an activity of God. As Barth's insight was developed, it became clear that mission has to do with the very nature of God.

South African Reformed theologian David Bosch, whose book *Transforming Mission* has had a profound influence on a reoriented missional theology, came to understand, along with others, that mission should be seen in the context of the doctrine of the Trinity, not the doctrine of the church or the doctrine of salvation. This shift means that mission is not primarily an activity of the church, but an attribute of God: *the Father sends the Son in the power of the Holy Spirit.* "God is a missionary God."[10]

Jürgen Moltmann draws out the implications of seeing mission at the very heart of who God is: "It is not the church that has a mission of salvation to fulfil to the world; it is the mission of the Son and the Spirit through the Father that includes the church."[11]

Mission as an attribute of God is not a theological innovation; it is central to the biblical witness. The following brief citations are among the many instances of New Testament witness to the sending God:

- [Jesus said,] "Whoever welcomes me welcomes not me but the one who sent me" (Mark 9:37).
- God did not send the Son into the world to condemn the world, but in order that the world might be saved through him (John 3:17).
- [Jesus said,] "The works that the Father has given me to complete, the very works that I am doing, testify on my behalf that the Father has sent me" (John 5:36).
- [Jesus said,] "You know me, and you know where I am from. I have not come on my own. But the one who sent me is true, and you do not know him. I know him, because I am from him, and he sent me" (John 7:28–29).
- [Jesus prayed,] "And this is eternal life, that they may know you, the only true God, and Jesus Christ whom you have sent. . . . for the words that you gave me I have given to them, and they have received them and know in truth that I come from you; and they have believed that you sent me" (John 17:3, 8).
- [Jesus prayed,] "As you have sent me into the world, so I have sent them into the world" (John 17:18).

- [The risen Jesus said to his disciples,] "Peace be with you. As the Father has sent me, so I send you." When he had said this, he breathed on them and said to them, "Receive the Holy Spirit" (John 20:21–22).
- [Peter preached,] "When God raised up his servant, he sent him first to you, to bless you by turning each of you from your wicked ways" (Acts 3:26).

The Apostolic Church

"Send" (*apostellō*) is also used in the New Testament for the sending of the disciples and the sending of the community. The church is not the body that sends some of its members out as missionaries; the church is the body that *is sent* into the world by the triune God to follow in the divine mission. As we profess our belief in "one holy catholic apostolic church," we affirm the apostolic church as the sent church, sent to bear witness to the gospel in fidelity to the apostolic faith. Barth emphasizes that the church's task "is comprehensively and decisively a service of mission and therefore a ministry *ad extra*. . . . [The church] stands in service of those who in fact live in the world without God and their fellows, and therefore in forfeiture of their own true selves. To such it is sent."[12]

The church is sent by God though Christ in the power of the Spirit to participate in God's active mission in the world, bearing witness to what God has done, is doing now, and promises to do in the future toward which we are drawn. The church's sending to participate in the *missio Dei* overcomes all simple and false distinctions between foreign mission, national mission, and local mission, between speaking and acting, between evangelism and justice, between praying and working, between giving and receiving. The whole church is sent to bear witness to the whole gospel in the whole world. A missional congregation, a missional classis or presbytery, a missional denomination lives not for itself, but for the world that God loved so much that he sent the Son into the world that it might have life. Mission is the center of the church's life, not one of the church's many programs. As Swiss Reformed theologian Emil Brunner puts it, "The church exists by mission just as fire exists by burning."[13]

Yet we know that in some congregations the fires are burning low. Thus the call for the church's continuing conversion. Serious, sustained attention to the gospel—theology—is critical at this point. For Barth, theology is central to mission:

> In theology the community gives a critical account, both to itself and to the world which listens with it, of the appropriateness or otherwise of its praise of God, its preaching, its instruction, its evangelistic and missionary work, but also of the activity which cannot be separated from these things, and therefore its witness in the full and comprehensive sense.[14]

The church, not immune to self-deception, can effortlessly convince itself that the myriad activities that fill its life are all "mission" and that the multiplication of activities qualifies the church as "missional."

Calling everything "mission" debases the word and minimizes actual mission. A generation ago, John Fry's insightful book, *The Trivialization of the United Presbyterian Church*, observed, "A transformation of mission has occurred, from a task God has given the church to do into a characteristic of the church's being. . . . In this way mission becomes equivalent to what the church does and is the sum of everything the church does: by definition."[15] God sends the church beyond itself to participate in mission to those who need the church's service of proclamation, compassion, and justice. The church is also called to many faithful ministries within itself, of course: worship, study, fellowship, pastoral care, and more. However, these necessary endeavors should not be confused with mission. When everything the church does is called mission, the church easily deceives itself and the *missio Dei* is buried under the weight of church programs designed to meet the needs of church members.

Mission in North America

Throughout the nineteenth and into the twentieth century, mission was characterized by the expansion of Christianity into Africa, Asia, and other "non-Christian" parts of the world. Bosch notes that this older understanding of mission was viewed as saving souls, or as introducing people from the East and South to the blessings of the West, or as the expansion of the church, or as the transformation of the world into the kingdom of God. In all cases, mission was conceived as an activity of the church in which mission was exported to faraway places. Today, there is a growing realization that the West is itself a mission field. Rather than only sending missionaries to bring the gospel to other lands, a crucial missional task of the church is to bring the gospel to a North American culture that is increasingly distanced from it.

One apparent result of the disestablishment of the church is the increasing number of Americans who do not know the narrative of God's redemptive engagement with the world, who do not experience the liberating grace of Christ, who are not embraced within the communion of the Holy Spirit. At the same time, American society continues to struggle with race, economic dislocation, medical care, natural disasters, crime, and a range of other issues that diminish human life. God's mission of human redemption embraces the whole world, and American churches have a missional calling to the whole world, including North America. The growth of congregational mission teams to Central America and the Caribbean, Africa, and Asia is commendable, but can become one more instance of the church sending a few to other places. The deeper challenge is for the whole congregation to know that it is sent into mission in its own place.

What form might the church's mission take if it responded to its missional calling? Barth provides an intriguing exposition of the community's missional calling, in which the inner life of the community of faith impels it into the world, serving the world in speech and action. The following excerpts can indicate only the surface of Barth's thought, but they provide an entry into the church's specific, concrete thinking about its missional service in its specific, concrete location:

We begin with the service in which the community acts by its speech.

1. "We indicate a special service when we maintain that it is our office to praise God. . . . When [the community] praises God its particular concern is to set up that banner, to raise a standard, to lift up an escutcheon, in the ministry of its witness. The community's ministry of witness has to fill a yawning gap in the world."[16]

2. "Within it, yet also independently alongside, there belongs also the explicit proclamation of the Gospel in the assembly of the community, in the midst of divine service, where it is also heard directly or indirectly by the world."[17]

3. "Another basic form of the church's service [is] the instruction which is to be given to the community, first to its own members, but also to the world at large. . . . To attest to the Gospel in the world, there is serious though not exclusive need in both speaking and hearing of definite information which it is the duty of the community to impart to both the young and old, the educated and uneducated, within it."[18]

4. "We come to the speech and action of the community which are for the most part directed outwards to the world, and are therefore characteristically apostolic, when we turn to the task which might be and is excellently summed up in the term 'evangelisation.'. . . It is the particular task, undoubtedly laid upon the Church in every period, of ministering the Word of God to the countless men and women who theoretically ought to have heard and accepted and responded to it, but who in fact have not really done so."[19]

5. "The other function in which the community has to speak apostolically in the more specific sense is that of mission in the narrower sense . . . in which sending or sending out to the nations to attest the Gospel is the very root of the existence and therefore the whole ministry of the community."[20]

6. "In relation to the speaking community we come finally to the ministry of theology . . . There would be no theology if there were no service specially committed to the witness of word. . . . In solidarity with the community theology in all its movements must always have in view the surrounding world and its thought and aspiration, its action and inaction."[21]

There is a second series of forms of service in which it is predominantly action.

7. "As is perhaps fitting, we begin with prayer. . . . It is absolutely indispensible in the accomplishment of the action required of the community."[22]

8. "By the cure of souls we understand the activity of the community as . . . the participation of the one in the particular past, present, and future of the other, in his particular burdens and afflictions, but above all in his particular promise and hope in the singularity of his existence as created and sustained by God."[23]

9. "To the active witness of the community there belong the production and existence of definite personal examples of Christian life and action."[24]

10. "In diaconate the community explicitly accepts solidarity with the least of little ones, with those who are in obscurity and are not seen, with those who are pushed to the margin and perhaps the very outer margin of the life of human society. . . . In its distinctive task of giving help to the needy in the totality of their human existence cannot be undertaken in the long run unless the community realizes that the need of individuals is . . . grounded in certain disorders of the whole of human life in society."[25]

11. "The action of the community in the service of its witness is a prophetic action, i.e., an action based on perception into the meaning of the current events, relationships, and forms both of its own history and that of the world around in their positive and negative connexion to the immanent kingdom of God."[26]

12. "The Christian community acts in the fact that it establishes fellowship . . . one of the uniting factors in the common life of humanity . . . [regarding especially] the racial question . . . cultural differences . . . economic class."[27]

This lengthy citation of Barth's work is not meant to provide a complete missional checklist (although one could do worse) but to indicate the necessity of specific attention to the shape of a missional church. The missional stream of the Reformed tradition does not run deep, but it has provided living water for an evolving Reformed missional theology. Karl Barth, David Bosch, Darrell Guder, George Hunsberger, Craig Van Gelder, and other Reformed theologians offer the church a theologically sound vision of the future shape of the church and the ongoing life of the Reformed tradition.

A Living Tradition

The continuing reformation of the church . . . *ecclesia reformata semper reformanda secundum verbum Dei* . . . the church reformed, always to be reformed in accordance with the word of God. The Reformed tradition is not a relic of the past, but a living tradition that remains true to itself by continuous openness to the movement of the Spirit through the living Word of God. Openness to the Holy Spirit may lead to the honest recognition that the missional history of Reformed churches has not always been faithfully attentive to God's mission in the world.

The Reformed confessional tradition gives scant attention to the mission of the church. Sixteenth-century Reformed confessions simply do not touch upon the matter. Similarly, seventeenth-century confessions neglect the mission of the church (although the Westminster Larger Catechism's section on the positive duties required by the Ten Commandments set forth an explicit social ethic). The glaring absence of attention to mission was addressed early in the twentieth century when the Presbyterian Church in the United States of America amended the Westminster Confession of Faith by adding a chapter, "Of the Gospel of the Love of God and Missions."[28] Even then, however, the new chapter was confined to international evangelism, "the extension of the Kingdom of Christ throughout the whole earth."

It was not until the mid-twentieth century that Reformed confessions began to deal with mission in a more complete sense. The Confession of 1967 devoted a section to "The Mission of the Church," but even then, mission was seen only through the lens of reconciliation.[29] More recently, however, the Christian Reformed Church has given voice to the church's missional calling in its statement, "Our World Belongs to God."

> Joining the mission of God,
> the church is sent
> with the gospel of the kingdom
> to call everyone to know and follow Christ
> and to proclaim to all
> the assurance that in the name of Jesus
> there is forgiveness of sin
> and new life for all who repent and believe.
> The Spirit calls all members
> to embrace God's mission
> in their neighborhoods
> and in the world:
> to feed the hungry,
> bring water to the thirsty,
> welcome the stranger,
> clothe the naked,
> care for the sick,
> and free the prisoner.

We repent of leaving this work to a few,
for this mission is central to our being.[30]

What accounts for the relative silence of the Reformed tradition and its confessional statements about the full missional calling of the church? An answer to the question begins with the recognition that Reformed Christians have never believed that their ecclesial tradition possesses the whole truth at any moment in history. Instead, it has been a central characteristic of the Reformed tradition that it is open to the promise of "being reformed in accordance with the word of God" at any and every moment of the church's life. At any and every moment in the life of the church, the Spirit may lead us to the in-breaking of a new calling or the recovery of an old vocation. At this time in the life of North American Reformed churches, it may be that "to be Reformed" is to be open to new missional possibilities that God is placing before us. As we attend to Scripture and the deep tradition of the church, we may be confronted by the Word that calls us to the continuing reformation of our faithfulness to the gospel.

Alasdair MacIntyre tells us what we may already sense:

> A living tradition, then, is an historically extended, socially embodied argument, and an argument precisely in part about the goods which constitute that tradition. . . . [A]n adequate sense of tradition manifests itself in a grasp of those future possibilities which the past has made available to the present.[31]

Only rarely does any tradition experience a decisive rupture with its past; more often, a tradition discovers neglected resources in its past that lead to new insights for present faith and faithfulness. In that spirit, the Reformed tradition continues a lively conversation through time and in actual churches about the evolving shape of the tradition's commitments.

As the conversation continues, Reformed theologian Jürgen Moltmann, whose recovery of the neglected eschatological thrust of Christian faith began with *Theology of Hope*, alerts the church to a predicament, expressed in "the crisis of relevance and the crisis of identity."

> The more theology and the church attempt to become relevant to the problems of the present day, the more deeply they are drawn into the crisis of their own Christian identity. The more they attempt to assert their identity in traditional dogmas, rights and moral notions, the more unbelievable and irrelevant they become. This double crisis can be more accurately described as the identity-involvement dilemma.[32]

The Reformed tradition cannot remain in its past, merely repeating insights developed by previous generations. Neither can it abandon its faithful past in pursuit of current enthusiasms. The church is "to be reformed," not simply "changed." Furthermore, the church's reformation is to be in accordance with the word of God, not the siren call of contemporary culture. "Do not believe every spirit," says John, "but test the spirits to see whether they are from God; for many false prophets have gone out into the world" (1 John 4:1).

The Reformed tradition must be faithful to the best of its past, maintaining its clear Christian identity, while bringing insights to bear on contemporary realities. As we navigate the shoals of our "identity-involvement dilemma," the "historically extended, socially embodied argument" of the Reformed tradition is our best assurance of fidelity to the Holy Spirit.

1. David James Duncan, *The Brothers K* (New York: Bantam Books, 1992), pp. 576ff.
2. Carl E. Braaten, *The Flaming Center: A Theology of the Christian Mission* (Philadelphia: Fortress Press, 1977), p. 15.
3. Darrell L. Guder, *The Continuing Conversion of the Church* (Grand Rapids: Eerdmans, 2000), p. 150.
4. Calvin, "The Necessity of Reforming the Church," in *Calvin: Theological Treatises*, p. 183.
5. Ibid., p. 188.
6. Ronald S. Wallace, *Calvin, Geneva and the Reformation* (Eugene, OR: Wipf & Stock, 1998), p. 113.
7. Ibid.
8. Calvin's Commentary on Matthew 12:7, quoted in William J. Bouwsma, *John Calvin: A Sixteenth-Century Portrait* (New York: Oxford University Press, 1988), p. 192.
9. Hall, *An Awkward Church*, Occasional Paper No. 5 (Louisville: Office of Theology and Worship, 1993), p. 5.
10. David Bosch, *Transforming Mission* (Maryknoll, NY: Orbis Books, 1991), p. 390.
11. Moltmann, *The Church in the Power of the Spirit*, p. 64.
12. Barth, *Church Dogmatics*, IV.3.2., p. 832.
13. Emil Brunner, *The Word and the World* (New York: Charles Scribner's Sons, 1983), p. 108.
14. Barth, *Church Dogmatics*, IV.3.2., p. 879.
15. John Fry, *The Trivialization of the United Presbyterian Church* (New York: Harper & Row, 1975), p. 23.
16. Barth, *Church Dogmatics*, IV.3.2., p. 865.
17. Ibid., IV.3.2., p. 867.
18. Ibid., IV.3.2., p. 870.
19. Ibid., IV.3.2., pp. 872ff.
20. Ibid., IV.3.2., p. 874.
21. Ibid., IV.3.2., pp. 879, 882.
22. Ibid., IV.3.2., p. 882.
23. Ibid., IV.3.2., p. 885.
24. Ibid., IV.3.2., p. 887.
25. Ibid., IV.3.2., p. 892.
26. Ibid., IV.3.2., p. 895.
27. Ibid., IV.3.2., pp. 898-900.
28. *Book of Confessions*, 6.187-6.190.
29. Ibid., 9.31-9.47.
30. "Our World Belongs to God," 41.
31. MacIntyre, *After Virtue*, pp. 222ff.
32. Moltmann, *The Crucified God* (New York: Harper & Row, 1973), p. 7.

Additional Titles by Joseph D. Small

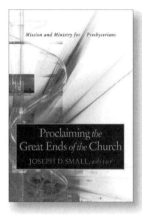

Prominent Presbyterian pastors and leaders address each of the Great Ends of the Church in sermons that both challenge and uplift readers. These sermons focus the church's understandings of its purpose and inspire us to dedicate ourselves to the church's work in the world. This is a book that every Presbyterian should know and is ideal for study by church groups and sessions.
$16.95
978-0664503079

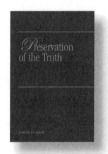

$16.95
978-1571532114

$14.95
978-1571530530

$12.95
978-1571531469

To order call the Presbyterian Distribution Service
at 800.524.2612 or visit store.pcusa.org

161